Security Clearance Issues, Problems, Denials and Revocations

(If you have a security clearance with no issues, then you don't need this book. If, however, you are worried about any aspect of your security clearance, then you absolutely need this book!)

By Attorney Ronald C. Sykstus*

225 Pratt Avenue

Huntsville, Alabama 35801

Offices located in Alabama,

Mississippi, and Tennessee

www.bondandbotes.com

*Admitted to Practice: Alabama;

Illinois; Tennessee; Washington,

D.C.; U.S. Courts of Appeals for

Veterans Claims; U.S. Tax Court.

Board Certified in Consumer

Bankruptcy Law by the American

Board of Certification

CONTENTS

Introduction

According to government statistics, for the past several years, on a yearly basis there are more than 4.3 million people nationwide who hold some level of security clearance.[1] Of this figure, approximately 3.5 million security clearances are held by government employees. The other million or so are held by government contractors or someone doing some type of work for the government but not employed by the government. For the overwhelming majority of these jobs, having a security clearance—which, in a nutshell, allows access to classified material—is a mandatory requirement for the job itself. If someone cannot get a clearance or has a clearance, but loses it, that generally means the job is no longer available to that person. For a small minority of people who have jobs that require clearances, and who either cannot get the clearance they need, or the clearance is subsequently suspended or revoked, their employer may offer them a position that entails non-classified work only, without the need of a clearance. In my experience, this does not happen often, so it is not something to count on.

My purpose of this book is right in the title. If you or your loved ones do not need a security clearance for your job, then don't even bother to read this book. Also, if you have a security clearance already, things are going swimmingly well with your job and your clearance, and there are no outside factors impinging upon you, likewise, you do not need to read this book.

---

[1] https://www.usatoday.com/story/news/2017/06/06/who-has-security-clearance/102549298/

This book is meant for people with security clearance concerns, issues, problems, denials, and revocations. In my law practice, I meet and speak with these people daily. For someone who has just landed his or her dream job with great pay and now is required to submit for a clearance and has worries and concerns, this book is for you. For someone who is already in his or her dream job, doing gratifying and well-paying work, whose clearance is now in jeopardy along with their job, this book is for you.

I live in Huntsville, Alabama, in the northern part of the state. Our offices are located throughout Alabama, and I work throughout the northern part of our state. Huntsville is the home of Redstone Arsenal, which always increases jobs during base realignments. And while it does not have a great number of active duty military, the civilian government and contracting community here is very large and robust. This is due to the fact that the Space and Missile Command is here, NASA is here, and the Materiel Command is here. As a result, there is a huge contingent of civilian government employees and an even larger number of civilian contractor employees who work directly for the government. All of these people need clearances for these great-paying and long-lasting jobs. Outside of Washington, D.C., our area probably has the most government employees and contractors in a concentrated area in the country.

I previously served on active duty with the U.S. Army Judge Advocate General's Corps with the U.S. Army Trial Defense Service. One of my jobs was to work with active-duty soldiers who were fighting security clearance problems and revocation hearings. I represented soldiers both at Fort McClellan, Alabama, in Anniston, Alabama, and at Redstone Arsenal, Alabama. Since I did so many of these defense cases and helped soldiers with clearances, it is something that I have continued to do as a civilian lawyer.

One of the things I like about this area of practice is that it is so meaningful to help someone get or keep his or her security clearance so that they can have or continue one of these great-paying jobs. If I was not a private lawyer here in North Alabama, there is no doubt that I would need a clearance to be able to live the kind of lifestyle I want for myself and my family. As a result, I carry the weight and worry of my clients who are worried about their security clearance and whether they will be able to get or keep the kind of job they want and, most often, need. I am fortunate to be able to represent clients who have clearance issues all over the United States and the world.

My law firm website is www.SecurityClearanceDefenseLawyer.com. I am available by phone anytime at 256-713-0221 or by email at rsykstus@bondnbotes.com

So, what is the purpose of this book? I have had so many people approach me who do not know where to turn when they are worried about their clearance and or potential problems or concerns or revocations. As a result, I thought it would be a good idea to put together a broad spectrum of the issues I see so that someone who is worried late at night or on the weekend can get this book and at least get some peace of mind as they try to work through their situation and keep their job. I am still available by phone or email to help, but I hope this will be a good starting point for someone to be able to get some sleep and give their worries a rest.

CHAPTER 1
I Want a Security Clearance to Get a Good Job

Government jobs and civilian employment are, generally speaking, quite lucrative and can also provide long-term security for employees. No wonder these jobs are coveted! Believe me, there are many days I look back and think government employment would have been a good way to go! The problem is that these jobs, by and large, require access to classified material, and thus, the employee must have security clearance.

I get several calls each week from people asking me to help them get a security clearance so that they can apply for one of these good jobs. The system, however, does not work that way. If someone already has a clearance and is applying for a job, that is one thing. It is most often the case, however, that someone gets a job that requires a clearance and that person has to be put in for one. An individual cannot simply go out and get a security clearance on his or her own, free and clear of a job.

The starting point that probably makes the most sense here is to detour a bit and cover the language used in the security clearance world. Since it is driven by the government, acronyms rule the day, as one would expect. These are the ones to know, in addition to what I have already mentioned.

1. CAF – Central Adjudications Facility located at Fort Meade, Maryland.

2. JPAS – Joint Personnel Adjudications System – Centralized computer system that contains everything related to security clearances, centrally located at the CAF.

3. FSO – Facility Security Officer – Every government and private entity that deals with classified material has a FSO who serves as a central clearinghouse for that entity for any matter related to security clearance.

4. e-QIP – Electronic questionnaires for investigation processing – This is how the security clearance application now is completed by the applicant.

5. SF 86 – Standard form 86 – This is the actual form utilized by the government and located online under the e-QIP, which is where applicants fill out this form using that electronic questionnaire.

6. DSS – Defense Security Service – The Defense Security Service is an agency of the Department of Defense (DoD) located in Quantico, Virginia, with field offices throughout the United States. The Under Secretary of Defense for Intelligence provides authority, direction, and control over DSS. DSS provides the military services, defense agencies, thirty-one federal agencies, and approximately 13,500 cleared contractor facilities with security support services.

As far as the types of security clearances, the following is a list of what people need (and the types they can get) in order to have access to classified material and perform their jobs.

1. Types of Security Clearances

1. Confidential – lowest level – commonly referred to as CAC or Common Access Card – for commissary workers, child care, etc. – Allows for base access and presence on base (Note – lesser form is used for CAC card, SF 85, not as intrusive or exhaustive as SF 86 form).

2. Secret Clearance – Most government and contractor jobs require this one – once granted, reviewed every ten years if no intervening incident.

3. Top Secret – TS – Once granted, reviewed every five years if no intervening incident. TS requires a SSBI (Single Scope Background Investigation) which will include a polygraph. TS is the top-level clearance but there can be variants:

    TS-SCI – Sensitive Compartmented Information

    TS-SAP – Special Access Program

4. A clearance is good for twenty-four months after loss of employment if it is not suspended or revoked. After twenty-four months, applicants have to go through the full investigation process again to include submitting a SF 86 or SF 85, as required. NASA, TVA, and nuclear programs have a similar process but more limited due process rights. Ninety percent of what most applicants will see and deal with will be the DOD process described herein and not NASA, TVA, or nuclear.

In practical terms, the way the system works is that someone applies for a job that requires a security clearance. Now that he or she is "sponsored" by the employer for a job that requires access to classified material, the facility security officer (FSO) of that government agency or civilian employer will put that person in for a security clearance through the JPAS system. It is a slow process, but hopefully within a two- to four-month period, an interim clearance will be granted if there are no immediate background issues such as criminal convictions or derogatory information in the FBI database.

Once an interim clearance is granted, the person who received it is then free to work on classified material. The CAF does a detailed background check of the applicant's background to include marriage, family history, further criminal check, interviews with people who have known the applicant since the age of sixteen, drug and alcohol screening, and pulling and reviewing the three main credit reports for that individual from Experian, Transunion, and Equifax. This review also includes a formal sit-down meeting with an investigator from the DSS (Defense Security Service) who will transcribe the interview. For a TS clearance, the investigation will be a bit more detailed and invasive. In 60 percent or more of TS cases, the applicant will have to fly to Washington, D.C., to undergo a polygraph examination. This polygraph can be quite intrusive as well.

CHAPTER 2

So Who Gets a Security Clearance?

This is a good question and, at times, the answer feels like it is ordained from above. In reality, the government has set forth adjudicative guidelines for determining eligibility for access to classified information for all U.S. government civilian and military personnel, consultants, contractors, employees of contractors, licensees, certificate holders or grantees and their employees, and other individuals who require access to classified information. These guidelines apply to persons being considered for initial or continued eligibility for access to classified information, to include sensitive compartmented information (TS-SCI) and special access programs (TS-SAP), and are to be used by government departments and agencies and for all final clearance determinations. Government departments and agencies may also choose to apply these guidelines to analogous situations regarding persons being considered for access to other types of protected information.

A variant of these guidelines will also apply to NASA, TVA, and nuclear personnel and/or contractors, so it is wise to know exactly what type of entity a security clearance applicant is trying to work for and what specific guideline covers access to classified material for the specific entity or department before trying to get a security clearance or appealing a clearance denial or revocation.

Decisions regarding eligibility for access to classified information take into account factors that could cause a conflict of interest or place a person in the position of having to choose between his or her commitments to the United States, including the commitment to protect classified information, and any other compelling loyalty. Access decisions also take into account a person's reliability, trustworthiness, and ability to protect classified information. No coercive policing could replace the self-discipline and integrity of the person entrusted with the nation's secrets, and these traits are the most effective means of protecting them. When a person's life history shows evidence of unreliability or untrustworthiness, questions arise whether the person can be relied on and trusted to exercise the responsibility necessary for working in a secure environment where protecting classified information is paramount.

The preceding paragraph is directly from the directive on security clearances. The last portion discussing a person's life history is the important phrase; allowing the government to perform an exhaustive inquiry regarding a person's background.

The adjudicative process is an examination of a sufficient period of a person's life to make an affirmative determination that the person is an acceptable security risk. Eligibility for access to classified information is predicated upon the individual meeting these personnel security guidelines. The adjudication process is the careful weighing of a number of variables known as the whole-person concept. Available, reliable information about the person, past and present, favorable and unfavorable, should be considered in reaching a determination. In evaluating the relevance of an individual's conduct, the adjudicator should consider the following factors: the nature, extent, and seriousness of the conduct; the circumstances surrounding the conduct, to include knowledgeable participation; the frequency and decency of the conduct; the individual's age and maturity at the time of the conduct; the extent to which participation is voluntary; the presence or absence of rehabilitation and other permanent behavioral changes; the motivation for the conduct; the potential for pressure, coercion, exploitation, or duress; and the likelihood of continuation or recurrence.

Each case must be judged on its own merits, and final determination remains a responsibility of a specific department or agency. Any doubt concerning personnel being considered for access to classified information will be resolved in favor of the national security.

The ability to develop specific thresholds for action under these guidelines is limited by the nature and complexity of human behavior. The ultimate determination of whether the granting or continuing of eligibility for security clearance is clearly consistent with the interests of national security must be an overall common-sense judgment based upon careful consideration of the following guidelines, each of which is to be evaluated in the context of the whole person.

Guideline A: Allegiance to the United States

Guideline B: Foreign Influence

Guideline C: Foreign Preference

Guideline D: Sexual Behavior

Guideline E: Personal Conduct

Guideline F: Financial Considerations

Guideline G: Alcohol Consumption

Guideline H: Drug Involvement

Guideline I: Psychological Conditions

Guideline J: Criminal Conduct

Guideline K: Handling Protected Information

Guideline L: Outside Activities

Guideline M: Use of Information Technology Systems

Although adverse information concerning a single criterion may not be sufficient for an unfavorable determination, the individual may be disqualified if available information reflects a recent or recurring pattern of questionable judgment, irresponsibility, or emotionally unstable behavior. Notwithstanding the whole-person concept, pursuit of further investigation may be terminated by an appropriate adjudicative agency in the face of reliable, significant, disqualifying, adverse information.

When information of security concern becomes known about an individual who is currently eligible for access to classified information, the adjudicator should consider whether the person voluntarily reported the information, was truthful and complete in responding to questions, sought assistance and had followed professional guidance, where appropriate, resolved or appears likely to favorably resolve the security concern, has demonstrated positive changes in behavior and employment, should have his or her access temporarily suspended pending final adjudication of the information.

If, after evaluating information of security concern, the adjudicator decides that the information is not serious enough to warrant a recommendation of disapproval or revocation of the security clearance, it may be appropriate to recommend approval with the warning that future incidents of a similar nature may result in revocation of access.

All of this information is found in Department of Defense Directive number 5220.6, January 2, 1992. Stated on the top right corner of the government's most current version as of the date of the printing of this book is the following: "This version of DOD directive 5220.6 contains the revised adjudicative guidelines implemented for the Department of Defense by the Under Secretary of Defense for intelligence on August 30, 2006 and made effective for any adjudication in which a statement of reasons is issued on or after September 1, 2006.

Anyone who is facing an issue regarding his or her clearance, or has a concern, please make sure to double check the directive that the DOD or any other entity is using with regard to the clearance. As I previously mentioned in this book, most entities as they relate to a clearance will use this specific directive. A few other entities use different guidelines, so be sure you know the exact and most recent guideline/directive that will directly impact and affect your security clearance. This is very important! Know and get a complete copy of the correct, exact, and up-to-date directive or regulation that is being used on your specific security clearance!

Just a final side note here before we start the next chapter. It is of historical significance, but I also bring it up because people may still believe that this issue poses a problem. It affected a good number of people for several years, which is why I want to discuss the Smith Amendment. Originally enacted in 2000 and found at 10 U.S.C. 986, this law barred contractors and employees of the Department of Defense and military personnel from holding a security clearance if they had been convicted of a crime and served more than one year of incarceration. This law applied for **any** conviction if anyone was convicted of an offense and sentenced to at least one year in jail, regardless of whether they ever had to serve jail time. The effect of this law, enacted in 2000, caused many employees who already held a security clearance to lose their clearances. As a result, they lost their jobs even if they were convicted of an offense many years before or the issue had already been flushed out and vetted by the security clearance agencies. This law and bar to security clearances was removed by law effective January 1, 2008. Under this fact pattern, under the new law, the bar now is limited to individuals having access to special access programs, restricted data, or any other information commonly referred to as sensitive, compartmented information if they have been convicted in any court of the United States of a crime, sentenced to imprisonment for a term exceeding one year, and incarcerated as a result of that sentence for not less than one year. Even in those circumstances, however, the law allows a waiver in meritorious cases if there are mitigating factors.

CHAPTER 3

Standard Form (SF) 86

For almost everyone in the security clearance world, just the phrase "SF 86" sends chills down the spine. It is the equivalent of talking about the bar exam for lawyers or the CPA exam for accountants. It evokes that same kind of sentiment and nauseating type of reaction.

The government has revised this form a number of times over the past several years. You can assume, and you would be correct, that the revisions are not meant to favor the applicants for security clearances. In my estimation, all the changes and revisions are designed precisely to ferret out behavior and circumstances that would allow the government to preclude granting someone access to classified material or revoking a security clearance previously awarded.

As we discussed previously, the SF 86 is done online now through the e-QIP system. An applicant does not need to complete it at one sitting, and he or she is allowed to do it over several days. This is always good policy, for reasons we will discuss later. The current version of the SF 86 used by the government as of the date of this book is December 2010. The top left corner of the SF 86 specifically states that it is "Revised December 2010." If the SF 86 you are filling out is dated with a date other than December 2010, then these questions and page numbers may appear to you in a different format than what is referenced here. If that is the case, please pay even more attention to the questions and your specific and detailed answers because that means substantive changes have been made to the SF 86 by the government since the date of publication of this book. This December 2010 document contains two pages of instructions at the front, followed by 122 substantive pages to be completed, and then three final pages for signatures and releases for all manner of material to be provided to the government.

Let's start with the instructions.

Here is how the SF 86 begins; it certainly gives you a strong sense of the import and solemnity of the form and the process.

"All questions on this form must be answered **completely and truthfully** in order that the government may make the determinations described below on a complete record. Penalties for inaccurate or false statements are discussed below. **If you are a current civilian employee of the federal government**: failure to answer any questions completely and truthfully could result in an adverse personnel action against you, including loss of employment; with respect to sections 23, 27 and 29, however, neither your truthful responses or information derived from those responses will be used against you in a subsequent criminal proceeding." Note that the words in bold are exactly as set forth in this first paragraph of the instructions.

The instructions then go on to explain the purpose of the form. "This form will be used by the United States government in conducting background investigations, reinvestigations, and continuous evaluations of persons under consideration for, or retention of, national security positions as defined in 5 CFR 732, and for individuals requiring eligibility for access to classified information under Executive Order 12968. This form may also be used by agencies in determining whether a subject performing work for, or on behalf of, the government under a contract should be deemed eligible for logical or physical access when the nature of the work to be performed is sensitive and could bring about an adverse effect on national security."

"Providing this information is voluntary. If you do not provide each item of requested information, however, we will not be able to complete your investigation, which will adversely affect your eligibility for national security position, eligibility for access to classified information, or logical or physical access. It is imperative that the information provided be true and correct to the best of your knowledge. Any information that you provide is evaluated on the basis of its currency, seriousness, relevance to the position and duties, and consistency with all information about you. Withholding, misrepresenting, or falsifying information may affect your eligibility for access to classified information, eligibility for sensitive position, or your ability to obtain or retain federal or contract employment. In addition, withholding, misrepresenting, or falsifying information may affect your eligibility for physical and logical access to federally controlled facilities or information systems. Withholding, misrepresenting, or falsifying information may also negatively affect your employment prospects and job status, and the potential consequences include, but are not limited to, removal, debarment from federal service, loss of eligibility for access to classified information, or prosecution."

"This form is a permanent document that may be used as the basis for future investigations, eligibility determinations for access to classified information, to hold a sensitive position, suitability or fitness for contract employment, or eligibility for physical and logical access to federally controlled facilities or information systems. Your responses to this form may be compared with your responses to previous SF-86 questionnaires."

You can see that, with those several-paragraph explanations under the purposes of the form, this is far-reaching on many different fronts. It is an exhaustive search and review of someone's background, and, as I have seen with the number of cases for my own clients, these SF 86 questionnaires have a way of resurfacing and causing clearance issues ten, twenty, or even thirty years down the road.

The instruction form describes the investigative process. It states, "Background investigations for national security positions are conducted to gather information to determine whether you are reliable, trustworthy, good conduct and character, and loyal to the US. The information that you provide in this form may be confirmed during the investigation. The investigation may extend beyond the time covered by this form, when necessary to resolve issues. Your current employer may be contacted as part of the investigation, although you may have previously indicated on applications or other forms that you do not want your current employer to be contacted. If you have a security freeze on your consumer credit report file, then we may not be able to complete your investigation, which can adversely affect your eligibility for a national security position. To avoid such delays, you should request that the consumer reporting agencies lift the freeze in these instances."

"In addition to the questions on this form, inquiry also is made about your adherence to security requirements, honesty and integrity, vulnerability to exploitation or coercion, falsification, misrepresentation, and any other behavior, activities, or associations that tend to demonstrate a person is not reliable, trustworthy, or loyal. Federal agency records checks may be conducted on your spouse, cohabitants, and immediate family members. After an eligibility determination has been completed, you may also be subject to continuous evaluation, which may include periodic reinvestigations to determine whether retention in your position is clearly consistent with the interests of national security."

After all of this, it is a wonder that anyone can get and/or keep a security clearance! Don't worry, however, we will get there through this book and hopefully put your worries and concerns to rest!

The instruction form also discusses the personal interview process. It states that some investigations will include an interview with you as a routine part of the investigative process. The investigator may ask you to explain your answers to questions on the form. This provides you the opportunity to update, clarify, and explain information on your form more completely, often assisting in completing your investigation. It is imperative that the interview be scheduled immediately after you are initially contacted. Postponements will delay the processing of the investigation, and declining to be interviewed may result in the investigation being delayed or canceled.

For the interview, a person will be required to provide photo identification, such as a valid driver's license. He or she may also be required to provide other documents to verify identity, as instructed by the investigator. These documents may include certification of any legal name change, Social Security card, passport, and birth certificate. The person may also be asked to provide documents regarding information that is provided on the SF 86, or about other matters requiring specific attention. These matters include alien registration or naturalization documents, delinquent loans or taxes, bankruptcies, judgments, liens, or other financial obligations; agreements involving child support or custody, alimony, or other property settlements, arrests, convictions, probation and/or parole, or other matters described in court records.

The instructions note that the final determination on an applicant's eligibility for a national security position is the responsibility of the federal agency that requested the investigation and the end agency that conducted the investigation. It notes that the applicant will be provided the opportunity to explain, refute, or clarify any information before a final decision is made, if an unfavorable decision is considered. It further notes that the government does not discriminate on the basis of race, color, religion, sex, national origin, disability, or sexual orientation when granting access to classified information.

Finally, the instructions reference the main concern that everyone has when filling out the SF 86. The instructions specifically spell out penalties for inaccurate or false statements; the United States Criminal Code (title 18, section 1001) provides that knowingly falsifying or concealing a material fact is a felony which may result in fines and/or up to five years imprisonment. In addition, federal agencies generally fire, do not grant a security clearance, or disqualify individuals who have materially and deliberately falsified these forms, and this remains a part of the permanent record for future placements. Your prospects of placement or security clearance are better if you answer all questions truthfully and completely. You will have adequate opportunity to explain any information you provide on the form and to make your comments part of the record.

CHAPTER 4

Standard Form (SF) 86 in Detail

Now that we know the lay of the land with regard to the SF 86, I will now cover it in detail—specifically, the problem questions on the form—and discuss issues that I have seen throughout the years. We have already seen in the instruction section the absolute importance that the government places on true, full, and complete disclosure. The instructions also provide that the government can always look back at older SF 86s to compare them to more recent ones that are completed and submitted. As a result, what I always tell my clients is that the first submission of your SF 86 is your story and, whatever your story is, it is my advice that it must stay consistent throughout. Any future changes or corrections on a subsequent SF 86 can, and probably will, come back to haunt you.

As a general rule, I am rarely, if ever, concerned about actual behavior or past troubling issues that are reported on an SF 86. What is more concerning to me, and where I see my clients get into problems, is when behavior is not fully disclosed at the outset, or corrected later. It is more often a failure to disclose or an intentional omission of information that causes people security clearance problems, rather than the behavior itself. That is not to say that the government will not explore concerning behavior in relation to the granting of a security clearance. But it is almost always easier to explain away the behavior rather than having to respond to why the government thinks you failed to adequately and truthfully answer the questions posed, especially after being told how important truthful and full disclosure is before you started to complete the form.

So, with that said, we will simply walk through the SF 86, page by page, and address the questions that, in my experience, can trip people up. Most of the SF 86 is not complicated—standard information that individuals already know about themselves—and will not provide any cause for concern. This is true as it relates to previous residences, marital status, acquaintances, etc. Sometimes, clients will be concerned with problem areas and ask me for counsel. In that context, I always ask my clients to give me the exact question they are worried about and the proposed answer they would like to submit. From there, we can tweak it and put it in the best possible light. Sometimes, these very same clients will send me their entire completed SF 86 and not point out the problem questions! I always tell my clients that I do not need to review the entire SF 86 since most of it contains rote, simple information that will not cause an issue. I am always concerned with problem questions that are concerning to my clients.

One last thing before we get started. The SF 85—for lower-level clearances such as a CAC card—contains many of the same questions as the SF 86. Because the clearance level is lower, the document is shorter. Many of the same concerns that people have in the SF 86, however, will also be found in the SF 85. As a result, regardless of which form you are required to fill out, this information can be used interchangeably for your benefit as well.

A. Problem Questions I See for My Clients on the SF 86

The questions that I point out in this section are the ones that I have specifically discussed with my clients. There are likely other questions that can give rise to problems or concerns for readers of this book, but all I am doing here is pointing out the issues that I have observed.

1. Section 10 – Dual/Multiple Citizenship & Foreign Passport Information

Page 4 – 10.1 – Do you now or have you **EVER** held dual/multiple citizenships? Yes or No.

Page 4 – 10.2 – Have you **EVER** been issued a passport (or identity card for travel) by a country other than the U.S.? Yes or No.

Note that both of these questions use the word **EVER** and not the last seven or ten years like other questions. Pay attention anytime you see the word **EVER,** which will usually be capitalized and bold, but sometimes it will just be in lowercase. You can get tripped up here very easily with a careless mistake. Also, be aware that if you answer yes to either of these questions, in all likelihood, an issue will be raised as far as the government's concerns. So you will need to be able to readily prove your history.

2. Section 13 – Employment Activities

Section 13 on page 13 of the SF 86 deals with employment activities. I have seen a number of clients get tripped up in this area. The instruction paragraph tells applicants to list all employment activities, including unemployment and self-employment, beginning with the present and working back ten years. The entire time period must be accounted for without breaks. If the employment activity was military duty, there is a separate area to show each change of military duty station.

Page 20 – 13A.5 – Provide the reason for leaving the employment activity. For this employment have any of the following happened to you in the last seven years? Fired, quit after being told you would be fired, left by mutual agreement following charges or allegations of misconduct, or left by mutual agreement following notice of unsatisfactory performance. Yes or no.

State the reason for the end of employment in the employment departure date. Were you fired? Did you quit after being told you would be fired, leave by mutual agreement following charges of allegations of misconduct, or leave by mutual agreement following notice of unsatisfactory performance? Provide the reasons or charges and the dates regarding these allegations.

Page 20 – 13A.6 – For this employment, in the last seven years have you received a written warning, been officially reprimanded, suspended, or disciplined for misconduct in the workplace such as a violation of security policy? Yes or no. Provide the reasons for being warned, reprimanded, suspended, or disciplined in the month and year.

Page 29 – 13C – Have any of the following happened to you in the last seven years at any employment activities that you have not previously listed? Fired from a job? Quit a job after being told you would be fired? Have you left a job by mutual agreement following charges or allegations of misconduct? Left a job by mutual agreement following notice of unsatisfactory performance? Received a written warning, been officially reprimanded, suspended, or disciplined for misconduct in the workplace, such as violation of the security policy? Yes or no.

These employment questions are asked several different ways. If there is a misstatement or omission, then in all likelihood, it will come out, and there will be an allegation of a misstatement on the SF 86. I always tell my clients that if there is any possibility someone will say they were terminated or let go for any of these reasons, they must disclose it here or risk losing or being denied a clearance. I have seen a number of clients who answer no to these questions and then, when the government solicits information from the former employer, the former employer states that the applicant was terminated for cause and gives the reasons. Now my client has a misstatement on the SF 86 to deal with. It is much better to avoid this potential issue on the front end and explain what happened. Also, note that all these questions apply to military service of any type, including both active and reserve service. So the questions all apply and are the same. This goes for whether someone received **non-judicial punishment** of any type, counseling statements, or anything of that nature while in active or reserve military service. Answer the questions fully, completely, and honestly and, when in doubt, answer yes with an explanation. That is **always** the safer course.

3. Section 15 – Military History

Page 30 – Section 15.2 – Were you discharged from this instance of U.S. military service, to include reserves or National Guard? Yes or no.

Provide the type of discharge you received: Honorable; Dishonorable; Under Other Than Honorable Conditions; General; Bad Conduct; Other—provide type. **Provide the reasons for the discharge, if the discharge is other than honorable.**

Page 31 – Section 15.2 – **In the last seven years**, have you been subject to court-martial or other disciplinary procedure under the Uniform Code of Military Justice (UCMJ) such as Article 15, Captains Mast, Article 135 Court of Inquiry, etc.? Yes or no. Complete the following if you responded yes in the last seven years to the above. Provide the date of court-martial or other disciplinary procedure, provide a description of the UCMJ offenses for which you were charged, provide the name of the disciplinary procedure, provide the description of the military court or other authority in which you were charged, and provide a description of the final outcome of the disciplinary procedure such as found guilty, found not guilty, fine, reduction in rank, imprisonment, etc.

The important part to note about this section is that it covers **all** disciplinary procedure to include, importantly, nonjudicial punishment, which is any type of action short of a court-martial. As a result, this covers all disciplinary measures in the military within the last seven years.

4. Section 17 – Marital Status

Page 36 – Section 17 – The important thing to know about this section is that it covers current marriages, prior marriages, and cohabitation. With regard to prior marriages, the topics covered are divorce, annulment, widowed, or other former spouses. With regard to cohabitation, the section defines a cohabitant as a person with whom you share bonds of affection, obligation, or other commitment, as opposed to a person with whom you live with for reasons of convenience like a roommate. If applicable, complete the following about your cohabitant if your cohabitant was born outside of the United States and provide citizenship information. In this section, I advise applicants to be very exacting about all prior marriages and current cohabitation arrangements.

5. Section 19 – Foreign Contacts

Page 59 – Section 19 – Do you have, or have you had, close and/or continuing contact with a foreign national within the last seven years with whom you, or your spouse, or cohabitant are bound by affection, influence, common interests, and/or obligation? Include associates as well as relatives, not previously listed in Section 18. Yes or no. If yes, provide the full name of the foreign national. Provide approximate date of first contact. Provide approximate date of last contact. Provide methods of contact and check all that apply: in person, written correspondence, telephone, electronic such as email, text, chat room, etc. or other. Provide approximate frequency of contact; daily, weekly, monthly, quarterly, annually or other. Provide the nature of the relationship whether it is professional or business, personal, obligation, or other. Provide the country of citizenship, date of birth, place of birth, current address foreign national's current employer and employer address. Also asked, if this foreign national is affiliated with a foreign government, military, security, defense industry or intelligence service. In my experience, it is important that this type of information and foreign contact is disclosed thoroughly. In that same light, please be prepared to answer questions from the government investigator regarding all facets of any and all foreign contacts.

6. Section 20 – Foreign Activities

Page 63 – Section 20A.1 – Have you, your spouse, cohabitant or dependent children **EVER** had any foreign financial interests such as stocks, property, investments, bank accounts, ownership of corporate entities, corporate interests or businesses in which you or they have had direct control or direct ownership? Exclude financial interests in companies that are diversified mutual funds that are publicly traded on a U.S. exchange. If an applicant has these types of ownership interests, he or she will need to provide all of the detailed information regarding these foreign financial interests. This is especially important when applicants come from other countries. Regardless, please note that this question covers the entirety of a person's lifetime since it asked if someone has **ever** had these types of interest. Do not limit yourself to the last seven years with regard to this question.

Page 65 – Section 20A.2 – Have you, your spouse, cohabitant, or dependent children **EVER** had any foreign financial interests that someone controlled on your behalf? Yes or no. If yes, please note to whom this applies and provide the type of financial interest, the name and relationship of the person who holds the interest in the exact details of the interest itself.

Page 67 – Section 20A.3 – Have you, your spouse, cohabitant, or dependent children **EVER** owned, or do you anticipate owning, or plan to purchase real estate in a foreign country?

Page 69 – Section 20A.4 – As a US citizen, have you, your spouse, cohabitant, or dependent children **received in the past seven years,** or are eligible to receive in the future, any educational, medical, retirement, social welfare, or other such benefit from a foreign country?

Page 71 – Section 20A.5 – Have you **EVER** provided financial support for any foreign national?

Page 72 – Section 20B.1 – Have you in **the past seven years** provided advice or support to any individuals associated with a foreign business or other foreign organization that you have not previously listed as a former employer?

Page 73 – Section 20B.3 – Has any foreign national in **the past seven years** offered you a job, did you work as a consultant, or consider employment with them?

Page 74 – Section 20B.4 – Have you in **the past seven years** been involved in any other type of business venture with a foreign national not described above (own, co-own, serve as business consultant, provide financial support, etc.)?

Page 75 – Section 20B.5 – Have you in **the past seven years** attended or participated in any conference, trade shows, seminars, or meetings outside of the U.S.?

Page 76 – Section 20B.6 – Have you or any member of your immediate family in **the past seven years** had any contact with a foreign government, its establishment such as embassy, consulate, agency, military service, intelligence security service, etc. or its representatives, whether inside or outside the U.S.?

Page 77 – Section 20B.7 – Have you in **the past seven years** sponsored any foreign national to come to the U.S. as a student, for work, or for permanent residence?

Page 79 – Section 20B.8 – Have you **EVER** held political office in a foreign country?

Page 80 – Section 20C – Have you traveled outside the U.S. in **the last seven years**? If yes, has your travel in the last seven years been solely for US government business (i.e., no personal trips in conjunction with the official US government business)?

Page 81 – Section 20C – Complete the following if you responded yes to having traveled outside the US in the **last seven years** for other than solely U.S. government business. Provide information about all such trips made outside the United States including personal trips made in conjunction with U.S. government business. Provide information on the country visited, the exact dates of travel, the total of numbers of days involved in the visit, the exact purpose of the travel, and whether you were questioned, searched or otherwise detained or have any encounter with the police, or were you contacted by anyone, or did anyone show any excessive knowledge or undue interest in you, or were you threatened, coerced, or pressured in any way?

The questions regarding foreign travel and involvement are extensive. A security clearance applicant will want to be exacting and definitive with regard to all foreign travel outside of the United States.

7. Section 21 – Psychological and Emotional Health

Page 84 – Section 21 – Mental health counseling in and of itself is not a reason to revoke or deny eligibility for access to classified information or for a sensitive position, suitability or fitness to obtain or retain federal employment, fitness to obtain or retain contract employment, or eligibility for physical or logical access to federally controlled facilities or information systems. **In the last seven years**, have you consulted with a healthcare professional regarding an emotional or mental health condition or were you hospitalized for such a condition? Answer no if the counseling was for any of the following reasons and was not court ordered: strictly marital, family, grief not related to violence by you; or strictly related to adjustments from service in a military combat environment. Please respond to this question with the following additional instruction: victims of sexual assault have consulted with the healthcare professional regarding an emotional or mental health condition during this period strictly in relation to the sexual assault are instructed to answer no. Complete the following if you have responded yes to having consulted with a healthcare professional regarding a mental or emotional health condition or hospitalized for such condition and provide the dates of the counseling or treatment, the name of the healthcare professional, the telephone number of the healthcare professional and full address. Were you **EVER** admitted as an inpatient to the agency/organization where the counseling/treatment was provided?

Hopefully, these redundant questions haven't put you to sleep. I say that because the next several sections, specifically section 22 – police record, section 23 – illegal use of drugs and drug activity, section 24 – use of alcohol and section 26 – financial record, are the major problem areas where the questions get very invasive and these are the most common areas where people get tripped up and either end up being denied a clearance or having a clearance revoked. With that said, let's look at section 22, police record.

8. Section 22 – Police Record

Page 86 – Section 22.1 – Have any of the following happened? If yes, you will be asked to provide details for each offense that pertains to the actions that are identified below.

In the past seven years have you been issued a summons, citation, or ticket to appear in court in a criminal proceeding against you? Do not check if all the citations involved were traffic infractions where the fine was less than $300 and did not include alcohol or drugs.

In the past seven years have you been arrested by any police officer, Sheriff, Marshall or any other type of law enforcement official?

In the past seven years have you been charged, convicted, or sentenced of a crime in any court? Include all qualifying charges convictions or sentences and any federal, state, local, military or non-US court even if previously listed on this form.

In the past seven years have you been or are you currently on probation or parole?

Are you currently on trial or awaiting a trial on criminal charges? For every yes answer, provide the date of the offense and a description and answer whether the offense involved domestic violence or a crime of violence such as battery or assault against your child, dependent, cohabitant, spouse or former spouse or someone with whom you share a child in common? Involve firearms or explosives? Involve alcohol or drugs? Also provide the location where the offense occurred and whether you were arrested, summoned, cited or did you receive a ticket to appear as a result of this offense by any police officer, sheriff, marshal or any other type of law enforcement official. As a result of this offense were you charged, convicted, currently awaiting trial, and/or ordered to appear in court in a criminal proceeding against you? Provide the location of the court and provide all the charges brought against you for this offense, and the outcome of each charge defense, such as found guilty, found not guilty, charge dropped or "nolle pros," etc. If you were found guilty of, or pleaded guilty to a lesser offense, list separately both the original charge and the lesser offense.

You can see how broad and far-reaching these questions go as far as police record questions. You have also seen the request that covers the last seven years for many items. In the change that was made to the SF 86 by revision in December, 2010, the government attempted to put to rest the issues where someone answered no under the thought that he or she was only being asked to cover the last seven years. It is important to note exactly what the exact question is that you are responding to. Is it a question that covers just the last seven years or does it cover an entire lifetime and use the word **EVER**? In an effort to address this in a little more detail and to take away the argument from an applicant who said that he or she will have answered erroneously because they thought it just covered the last seven years, section 22.2 addresses these types of questions.

Page 90 – Section 22.2 – Other than those offenses already listed, have you **EVER** had the following happened to you? Yes or no.

Have you **EVER** been convicted in any court of the United States of a crime, sentenced to imprisonment for a term exceeding one year for that crime, and incarcerated as a result of that sentence for not less than one year? Include all qualifying convictions in federal, state, local, or military court, even if previously listed on this form.

Have you **EVER** been charged with any felony offense? Include those under the Uniform Code of Military Justice and non-military/civilian felony offenses.

Have you **EVER** been convicted of an offense involving domestic violence or a crime of violence, such as battery or assault, against your child, dependent, cohabitant, spouse, former spouse, or someone with whom you share a child in common?

Have you **EVER** been charged with an offense involving firearms or explosives?

Have you **EVER** been charged with an offense involving alcohol or drugs?

Note that the word "ever" is in bold and in capital letters. I can virtually guarantee you that there will be an issue and a problem with the security clearance if someone answers no to these questions that cover an entire lifetime. If the answer is yes, the form provides that you give the date of the offense, a description and whether the offense involved domestic violence, firearms or explosives, or alcohol or drugs. It also asked for the exact location of the charging court, the disposition, and as much detailed information about the charge as possible. You can also be assured that the government investigator will obtain an entire copy of the court file. One last item to note in this area is with regard to military offenses. If there was a military criminal offense charged as a felony under the Uniform Code of Military Justice, you must find that information and disclose that exactly and accurately. This also applies to any type of charge in the military where, even if it was not a court-martial charge and ended up as non-judicial punishment, this must be disclosed as well if the original charge was for a felony offense.

9. Section 23 – Illegal Use of Drugs and Drug Activity

The preliminary instructions to this section state that "neither your truthful responses nor information derived from your responses to this section will be used as evidence against you in a subsequent criminal proceeding." This particular section applies whether or not you are currently employed by the federal government. The following questions pertain to the illegal use of drugs or controlled substances or drug or controlled substance activity.

Page 93 – Section 23.1 – **In the last seven years**, have you illegally used any drugs or controlled substances? Use of a drug or controlled substance includes injecting, snorting, inhaling, swallowing, experimenting with, or otherwise consuming any drug or controlled substance. Yes or no. Complete the following if you answered yes to in the last seven years having illegally used a drug or controlled substance. Provide the type of drug and controlled substance by checking one of these. Cocaine or crack cocaine such as rock, freebase, etc. THC such as marijuana, weed, pot, hashish, etc. Ketamine such as special K, jet, etc. Narcotics such as opium, morphine, codeine, heroin, etc. Stimulants such as amphetamines, speed, crystal meth, ecstasy, etc. Depressants such as barbiturates, methaqualone, tranquilizers, etc. Hallucinogenic such as LSD, PCP, mushrooms, etc. Steroids such as the clear, juice, etc. Inhalants such as toluene, amyl nitrate, etc. Other – provide explanation.

For the usage of the drugs you noted, provide an estimate of the month and year first used, an estimate of the month and year of most recent use, the nature of use, frequency, and number of times used. Also, answer whether your use was while you were employed as a law enforcement officer, prosecutor, or courtroom official or while in a position directly or immediately affecting the public safety. Also answer yes or no as to whether the use was while possessing a security clearance.

Page 94 – Section 23.2 – **In the last seven years**, have you been involved in the illegal purchase, manufacture, cultivation, trafficking, production, transfer, shipping, receiving, handling, or sale of any drug or controlled substance? Yes or no. If yes, provide the type of drug or controlled substance, provide an estimate of the month and year of first involvement, provide an estimate of the month and year of most recent involvement, and provide the nature and frequency of activity. Also provide the reason why you engaged in the activity.

Page 95 – Section 23.3 – Have you **EVER** illegally used or otherwise been involved with a drug or controlled substance while possessing a security clearance other than previously listed?

Page 96 – Section 23.5 – **In the last seven years**, have you intentionally engaged in the misuse of prescription drugs, regardless of whether or not the drugs were prescribed for you or someone else? Yes or no. If yes, provide the name of the prescription drug that you misused, provide the dates of usage, provide the circumstances of usage and whether the involvement was while possessing a security clearance, and whether you are employed as a law enforcement officer, prosecutor, courtroom official, or while in a position directly or immediately affecting the public safety.

Page 97 – Section 23.6 – Have you **EVER** been ordered, advised, or asked to seek counseling or treatment as a result of your illegal use of drugs or controlled substances? Yes or no. If yes, have any of the following ordered, advised, or asked you to seek counseling or treatment as a result of your illegal use of drugs or controlled substances? Check all that apply. An employer, military commander, or employee assistance program; a medical professional; a mental health professional; or a court official/judge. Did you take action to receive counseling or treatment? If yes provide an explanation and provide the exact type of drug or controlled substance for which you were treated and provide the name of the treatment provider, the address of the treatment provider, the telephone number of the treatment provider along with exact dates of treatment. Did you successfully complete the treatment? Yes or no.

Page 99 – Section 23.7 – Have you **EVER** voluntarily sought counseling or treatment as a result of your use of a drug or a controlled substance? Yes or no. If yes, provide the exact type of drug or controlled substance for which you were treated, provide the name of the treatment provider and the full address along with a telephone number and whether you successfully completed treatment.

10. Section 24 – Use of Alcohol

Page 100 – Section 24.1 – **In the last seven years,** has your use of alcohol had a negative impact on your work performance, your professional or personal relationships, your finances, or resulted in intervention by law enforcement/public safety personnel? Yes or no. If the answer is yes to alcohol use having had a negative impact on your work performance, your professional and/or your personal relationships, your finances, or resulted in intervention by law enforcement/public safety personnel, provide the dates of involvement of use, provide the month and year when this negative impact occurred, provide the circumstances and the negative impact. Provide this information for each particular time this has occurred.

Page 101 – Section 24.2 – Have you **EVER** been ordered, advised, or asked to seek counseling or treatment as a result of your use of alcohol? Yes or no. (As an aside, look at the broad perspective of this question. If **anyone** has ever advised you or asked you to seek counseling or treatment, then the answer is yes.) If you answered yes to this question, then check all that have asked you to seek counseling or treatment: an employer, military commander or employee assistance program; a medical professional; a mental health professional; a court official/judge; or other. Did you take action to receive counseling or treatment? Yes or no. If you responded no, explain the reasons for not taking action to seek counseling or treatment. If you responded yes to having taken action to seek counseling or treatment, provide the dates of counseling or treatment, the name of the individual counselor or treatment provider, the full mailing address and phone number of the treatment provider, and respond yes or no as to whether you successfully completed the treatment.

Page 102 – Section 24.3 – Have you **EVER** voluntarily sought counseling or treatment as a result of your use of alcohol? Yes or no. If the answer is yes, provide the dates of counseling or treatment, the name of the individual counselor treatment provider, and the full address and phone number of the counseling/treatment provider. Also, answer yes or no as to whether you successfully completed the treatment.

Page 103 – Section 24.4 – Have you **EVER** received counseling or treatment as a result of your use of alcohol in addition to what you have already listed on this form? Yes or no. If the answer is yes, provide the dates of counseling or treatment, the name of the individual counselor treatment provider, and the full address and phone number of the counseling/treatment provider. Also, answer yes or no as to whether you successfully completed the treatment.

11. Section 25 – Investigations and Clearance Record

Page 104 – Section 25.1 – Has the U.S. government or a foreign government **EVER** investigated your background and/or granted you a security clearance eligibility/access? Yes or no.

Page 105 – Section 25.2 – Have you **EVER** had a security clearance eligibility/access authorization denied, suspended, or revoked?

12. Section 26 – Financial Record

Of all the areas on the SF 86 where security clearance applicants run into trouble, this is the number one problem area. Drugs, alcohol, and criminal background issues, all with varying degrees, fall into the number two slot. The financial problems, however, are the biggest area in which I see people run into issues. I have had judges and opposing government counsel also tell me this is the number one area that presents problems for security clearance applicants.

Page 106 – Section 26.1 – **In the last seven years,** have you filed a petition under any chapter of the bankruptcy code? Yes or no. If yes, state which chapter of the code; chapter 7, chapter 11, or chapter 13, and provide the Bankruptcy Court docket/account number. Also provide the date the bankruptcy was filed, the date the bankruptcy was discharged, the total amount of dollars involved in the bankruptcy, the name the case is recorded under, the name of the court involved, the address of the court involved, and the trustee name and address for the bankruptcy.

Page 107 – Section 26.2 – Have you **EVER** experienced financial problems due to gambling? Yes or no. If yes, provide the date range of the financial problems, and estimate of the amount of U.S. dollars of gambling losses, and a description of the financial problems due to gambling and if any actions were taken to rectify financial problems due to gambling.

Page 107 – Section 26.3 – **In the last seven years,** have you failed to file or pay federal, state, or other taxes when required by law or ordinance? Yes or no. If yes, did you fail to file or pay as required, or both?

Note whether it is specifically a failure to file, a failure to pay, or both. Provide the year you failed to file or pay your federal, state, or other taxes.

Provide the reason for your failure to file or pay required taxes, provide the federal, state, or other agency to which you failed to file or pay taxes, provide the type of taxes you failed to file or pay, provide the amount of the taxes, and note whether the taxes have been satisfied or not. Finally, provide a description of any actions you have taken to satisfy this debt, such as withholdings, frequency and amount of payments, etc. If you have not taken any actions, provide an explanation.

Page 108 – Section 26.4 – **In the last seven years,** have you been counseled, warned, or disciplined for violating the terms of agreement for a travel or credit card provided by your employer?

Page 109 – Section 26.6 – Other than previously listed, have any of the following happened to you? You will be asked to provide details about each financial obligation that pertains to the items identified below.

In the last seven years, you have been delinquent on alimony or child support payments.

In the last seven years, you had a judgment entered against you. Include financial obligations for which you were the sole debtor, as well as those for which you were a cosigner or guarantor.

In the last seven years, you had a lien placed against your property for failing to pay taxes or other debts. Include financial obligations for which you were the sole debtor, as well as those for which you were a cosigner or guarantor.

You are currently delinquent on any federal debt. Include financial obligations for which you are the sole debtor, as well as those for which you are a cosigner or guarantor.

For every item where you answered yes, please provide the name of agency/organization/individual to which the debt was owed, the dollar amount, the date the financial issue began, when it was resolved, and what actions you have taken to satisfy this debt, such as withholdings, frequency, amount of payment, etc. If you have not taken any actions, provide an explanation.

Page 111 – Section 26.7 – Other than previously listed, have any of the following happened? Yes or no.

In the last seven years, have you had any possessions or property voluntarily or involuntarily repossessed or foreclosed? Include financial obligations for which you were the sole debtor, as well as those for which you were a cosigner or guarantor.

In the last seven years, did you default on any type of loan? Include financial obligations for which you were the sole debtor, as well as those for which you were a cosigner or guarantor.

In the last seven years, did you have bills or debts turned over to a collection agency? Include financial obligations for which you were the sole debtor, as well as those for which you were a cosigner or guarantor.

In the last seven years, did you have any account or credit card suspended, charged off, or canceled for failing to pay as agreed? Include financial obligations for which you were the sole debtor, as well as those for which you were a cosigner or guarantor.

In the last seven years, were you evicted for non-payment?

In the last seven years, were your wages, benefits, or assets garnished or attached for any reason?

In the last seven years, have you been over 120 days delinquent on any debt not previously entered? Include financial obligations for which you were the sole debtor, as well as those for which you were a cosigner or guarantor.

Are you currently over 120 days delinquent on any debt? Include financial obligations for which you were the sole debtor, as well as those for which you were a cosigner or guarantor.

For each question that you answered yes to, please provide the name of agency organization or individual to which the debt is owed, describe exactly the surroundings regarding this issue and to which of the questions that it applies to. Please also provide the associated loan and account number, the type of property, the amount owed in U.S. dollars, the reason for the financial issue, the current status of the financial issue, the date the financial issue began, and the date the issue was resolved. If it was not resolved, describe the circumstances. If it was resolved, also describe those circumstances.

13. Section 27 – Use of Information Technology Systems

Page 113 – Section 27.1 – **In the last seven years,** have you illegally or without proper authorization accessed or did you attempt to access any information technology system? Yes or no. If yes, provide the date of the incident, a description of the nature of the incident or offense, the location where the incident took place, a description of the action against you—administrative, criminal, or other—taken as a result of this incident.

Page 113 – Section 27.2 – **In the last seven years,** have you illegally or without authorization modified, destroyed, manipulated, or denied others access to information residing on an information technology system or attempted any of the above? Yes or no. If yes, provide the date of the incident, a description of the nature of the incident, location where the incident took place, and a description of the action that was taken as a result of this incident.

Page 114 – Section 27.3 – **In the last seven years,** have you introduced, removed, or used hardware, software, or media in connection with any information technology system without authorization, when specifically prohibited by rules, procedures, guidelines, regulations or attempted any of the above? Yes or no. If yes, provide the date of the incident, a description of the nature of the incident, location where the incident took place, and a description of the action that was taken as a result of this incident.

14. Section 28 – Involvement in Non-Criminal Court Actions

Page 115 – Section 28 – **In the last ten years,** have you been a party to any public record civil court action not listed elsewhere on this form? Yes or no. If yes, provide the date of the civil action, provide the court name, provide the address of the court, and also provide a detailed nature of the action along with the description of the results of the action and the names of the principal parties involved in the action.

15. Section 29 – Association Record

Page 116 – Section 29.1 – Are you now or have you **EVER** been a member of an organization dedicated to terrorism, either with an awareness of the organization's dedication to that end, or with the specific intent to further such activities? Yes or no. If yes, provide the full name of the organization, the full address and location dates of involvement, all positions held, contributions made, and a full description of the nature of and reasons for your involvement with the organization.

Page 117 – Section 29.2 – Have you **EVER** knowingly engaged in any acts of terrorism? Yes or no. If yes, describe the nature and reasons for the activity and the dates of such activities.

Page 117 – Section 29.3 – Have you **EVER** advocated any acts of terrorism or activities designed to overthrow the U.S. government by force? Yes or no. If yes, describe the nature and reasons for the activity and the dates of such activities.

Page 118 – Section 29.4 – Have you **EVER** been a member of an organization dedicated to the use of violence or force to overthrow the United States government which engaged in activities to that end, with an awareness of the organization's dedication to that end or with the specific intent to further such activities? Yes or no. If yes, describe the nature and reasons for the activity and the dates of such activities.

Page 119 – Section 29.5 – Have you **EVER** been a member of an organization that advocates or practices commission of acts of force or violence to discourage others from exercising their rights under the U.S. Constitution or any state of the United States with the specific intent to further such action? Yes or no. If yes, describe the nature and reasons for the activity and the dates of such activities.

Page 120 – Section 29.6 – Have you **EVER** knowingly engaged in activities designed to overthrow the U.S. government by force? Yes or no. If yes, describe the nature and reasons for the activity and the dates of such activities.

Page 120 – Section 29.7 – Have you **EVER** been associated with anyone involved in activities to further terrorism? Yes or no. If yes, describe the nature and reasons for the activity and the dates of such activities.

B. Summation of SF 86 Questions

As you can see, the questions on the SF 86 are broad-reaching and incisive. As a broad and definitive general rule, I am almost always much more concerned with a misstatement on an SF 86 than I am with the actual behavior that worries an applicant for security clearance. I always advise my clients to carefully, thoughtfully, and completely answer the questions on the SF 86. A person only gets one chance at this, and if it is discovered that there was a misstatement, falsification, or omission, it is very difficult to recover from that and get a security clearance. I further advise my clients to, if at all possible, get professional legal assistance for any question that makes you concerned or uncomfortable. There are ways to thoughtfully, and in detail, answer questions to put the answers in the best possible light. Also, when you are answering questions that are of concern, find out all the underlying information that you can with regard to those areas. For instance, if you have outstanding debts, get your credit reports so you know exactly what the government is looking at. If it is for criminal issues that have happened in your past, get a complete copy of the criminal court file so you know exactly what transpired and what the outcome was. If the issue is alcohol or drugs, then get all your treatment records, notably looking for a satisfactory prognosis and/or good prognosis for the future once rehabilitation is completed. If there is a question as to why you left the job and whether it was under duress or being told that you would be terminated in lieu of resignation, learn all those underlying facts and get all the performance appraisals that you received prior to the termination or end of employment. Again, know and understand all the underlying issues for any troubling questions that you see so that the answers can be properly and thoroughly completed.

Chapter 5

DOD Directive 5220.6

As mentioned earlier in this book, the Department of Defense directive 5220.6 controls everything that relates to a clearance as far as what concerns the government may have with allowing an individual access to classified material. This book is being written with the version of the DOD directive 5220.6 that contains the revised adjudicative guidelines implemented for the Department of Defense by the Under Secretary of Defense for intelligence on August 30, 2006 and made effective for any adjudication in which a statement of reasons was issued on or after September 1, 2006. Under that provision, it is noted that the directive is number 5220.6 issued on January 2, 1992. Please note that if the government issues a statement of reasons and provides you with a different number or different version of the directive, then some or all of what is written here may not be applicable. Since, however, the government has been using the same version since January 2, 1992 with the revision of August 30, 2006, it is a pretty good bet that this specific directive will stay in use for a long time.

In this chapter, my aim is to go through each guideline where I have handled cases and helped applicants for security clearances to address the government's concerns, as provided for in the mitigation section.

Guideline A: Allegiance to the United States

The Concern. An individual must be of unquestioned allegiance to the United States. The willingness to safeguard classified information is in doubt if there is any reason to suspect an individual's allegiance to the United States.

Conditions that could raise a security concern and may be disqualifying include:

a) involvement in, support of, training to commit, or advocacy of any act of sabotage, espionage, treason, terrorism, or sedition against the United States of America;

b) association or sympathy with persons who are attempting to commit, or who are committing, any of the above acts;

c) association or sympathy with persons or organizations that advocate, threaten, or use force or violence, or use any other illegal or unconstitutional means, in an effort to:

   1. overthrow or influence the government of the United States or any state or local government;

   2. prevent Federal, state, or local government personnel from performing their official duties;

   3. gain retribution for perceived wrongs caused by the Federal, state, or local government;

   4. prevent others from exercising their rights under the Constitution or laws of the United States or of any state.

Conditions that could mitigate security concerns include:

a) the individual was unaware of the unlawfulness of the individual or organization and severed ties upon learning of these;

b) the individual's involvement was only with the lawful or humanitarian aspects of such an organization;

c) involvement in the above activities occurred for only a short period of time and was attributable to curiosity or academic interest;

d)   the involvement or association with such activities occurred under such unusual circumstances, or so much time has elapsed, that it is unlikely to recur and does not cast doubt on the individual's recurrent reliability, trustworthiness, or loyalty.

For this particular guideline, I have never seen an issue or had a case arise under this particular concern. It makes sense given that if there is a serious question about allegiance to the United States, a person won't even get out of the gate as far as being able to submit or apply for a security clearance. As a result, I won't waste the reader's time here talking about issues that I don't think any of us will see, except in very weird and contorted circumstances.

Guideline B: Foreign Influence

The Concern. Foreign contacts and interests may be a security concern if the individual has divided loyalties or foreign financial interest, may be manipulated or induced to help a foreign person, group, organization, or government in a way that is not in U.S. interests, or is vulnerable to pressure or coercion by any foreign interest. Adjudication under this Guideline can and should consider the identity of the foreign country in which the foreign contact or financial interest is located, including, but not limited to, such considerations as whether the foreign country is known to target United States citizens to obtain protected information and/or is associated with a risk of terrorism.

Conditions that could raise a security concern and may be disqualifying include:

a)   contact with a foreign family member, business or professional associates, friend, or other person who is a citizen of or resident in a foreign country if that contact creates a heightened risk of foreign exploitation, inducement, manipulation, pressure, or coercion;

b)   connections to a foreign person, group, government, or country that create a potential conflict of interest between the individual's obligation to protect sensitive information or technology and the individual's desire to help a foreign person, group, or country by providing that information;

c) counterintelligence information, that may be classified, indicates that the individual's access to protected information may involve unacceptable risk to national security;

d) sharing living quarters with a person or persons, regardless of citizenship status, if that relationship creates a heightened risk of foreign inducement, manipulation, pressure, or coercion;

e) a substantial business, financial, or property interest in a foreign country, or in any foreign-owned or foreign-operated business, which could subject the individual to heightened risk of foreign influence or exploitation;

f) failure to report, when required, association with a foreign national;

g) unauthorized association with a suspected or known agent, associate, or employee of a foreign intelligence service;

h) indications that representatives or nationals from a foreign country are acting to increase the vulnerability of the individual to possible future exploitation, inducement, manipulation, pressure, or coercion;

i) conduct, especially while traveling outside the U.S., which may make the individual vulnerable to exploitation, pressure, or coercion by a foreign person, group, government, or country.

Conditions that could mitigate security concerns include:

a) the nature of the relationships with foreign persons, the country in which these persons are located, or the positions or activities of those persons in that country are such that it is unlikely the individual will be placed in a position of having to choose between the interests of a foreign individual, group, organization, or government and the interests of the U.S.;

b) there is no conflict of interest, either because the individual's sense of loyalty or obligation to the foreign person, group, government, or country is so minimal, or the individual has such deep and longstanding relationships and loyalties in the U.S. that the individual can be expected to resolve any conflict of interest in favor of the U.S. interest;

c) contact or communication with foreign citizens is so casual and infrequent that there is little likelihood that it could create a risk for foreign influence or exploitation;

d) the foreign contacts and activities are on U.S. Government business or are approved by the cognizant security authority;

e) the individual has promptly complied with existing agency requirements regarding the reporting of contacts, requests, or threats from persons, groups, or organizations from a foreign country;

f) the value or routine nature of the foreign business, financial, or property interests is such that they are unlikely to result in a conflict and could not be used effectively to influence, manipulate, or pressure the individual.

This guideline actually poses a problem or potential issue for a number of prospective security clearance applicants. I see this guideline come up several times each year. Though different from Guideline C— foreign preference, which we will cover next—it is usually listed as an issue by the government jointly with foreign preference as well. The way I usually see the foreign influence cases is where the security clearance applicant has family members and friends in a foreign country or financial holdings such as bank accounts, land, etc. I have also seen cases where people simply have very close friends in foreign countries. Under the mitigation allowed in this guideline, it is important to show the relationships between the applicant and the people in the foreign countries and show the deep ties to the United States such as paying taxes here, buying a house here, investment accounts and bank accounts here, etc. There is no prohibition from having family in a foreign country, but the applicant needs to focus on the fact that he or she is tied into the United States, and any potential conflict between the foreign relationships in the United States can be expected to be resolved in favor of the United States' interest.

Guideline C: Foreign Preference

The Concern. When an individual acts in such a way as to indicate a preference for a foreign country over the United States, then he or she may be prone to provide information or make decisions that are harmful to the interest of the United States.

Conditions that could raise a security concern and may be disqualifying include:

a) exercise of any right, privilege, or obligation of foreign citizenship after becoming a U.S. citizen or through the foreign citizenship of a family member. This includes but is not limited to:

    1. possession of a current foreign passport;

    2. military service or a willingness to bear arms for a foreign country;

    3. accepting educational, medical, retirement, social welfare, or other such benefits from a foreign country;

    4. residence in a foreign country to meet citizenship requirements;

    5. using foreign citizenship to protect financial or business interest in another country;

    6. seeking or holding political office in a foreign country;

    7. voting in a foreign election;

b) action to acquire or obtain recognition of a foreign citizenship by an American citizen;

c) performing or attempting to perform duties, or otherwise acting so as to serve the interest of a foreign person, group, organization, or government in conflict with the national security interest;

d) any statement or action that shows allegiance to a country other than the United States: for example, declaration of intent to renounce United States citizenship; renunciation of United States citizenship.

Conditions that could mitigate security concerns include:

a) dual citizenship is based solely on parents' citizenship or birth in a foreign country;

b) the individual has expressed a willingness to renounce dual citizenship;

c) exercise of the rights, privileges, or obligations of foreign citizenship occurred before the individual became a U.S. citizen or when the individual was a minor;

d) use of a foreign passport is approved by the cognizant security authority.

e) the passport has been destroyed, surrendered to the cognizant security authority, or otherwise invalidated;

f) the vote in a foreign election was encouraged by the United States Government.

The way for applicants to work around the government's concerns regarding foreign preference is to expressly renounce any foreign preference. For instance, the applicant can submit a statement to the FSO that says that he or she renounces his or her dual citizenship. He or she can also turn in any foreign passports to the FSO, and any foreign documentation or ownership can be surrendered and proof of this surrender provided to the FSO.

Guideline D: Sexual Behavior

The Concern. Sexual behavior that involves a criminal offense, indicates a personality or emotional disorder, reflects lack of judgment or discretion, or which may subject the individual to undue influence or coercion, exploitation, or duress can raise questions about an individual's reliability, trustworthiness, and ability to protect classified information. No adverse inference concerning the standards in this Guideline may be raised solely on the basis of the sexual orientation of the individual.

Conditions that could raise a security concern and may be disqualifying include:

a) sexual behavior of a criminal nature, whether or not the individual has been prosecuted;

b) a pattern of compulsive, self-destructive, or high-risk sexual behavior that the person is unable to stop or that may be symptomatic of a personality disorder;

c) sexual behavior that causes an individual to be vulnerable to coercion, exploitation, or duress;

d) sexual behavior of a public nature and/or that reflects lack of discretion or judgment.

Conditions that could mitigate security concerns include:

a) the behavior occurred prior to or during adolescence and there is no evidence of subsequent conduct of a similar nature;

b) the sexual behavior happened so long ago, so infrequently, or under such unusual circumstances that it is unlikely to recur and does not cast doubt on the individual's current reliability, trustworthiness, or good judgment;

c) the behavior no longer serves as a basis for coercion, exploitation, or duress.

d) the sexual behavior is strictly private, consensual, and discreet.

All human beings have normal desires in this area, so it is possible to work around this type of behavior. I think the mitigation allowed under B, C, and D is particularly important. This especially holds true if the behavior is strictly private, consensual, and discreet.

Guideline E: Personal Conduct

The Concern. Conduct involving questionable judgment, lack of candor, dishonesty, or unwillingness to comply with rules and regulations can raise questions about an individual's reliability, trustworthiness, and ability to protect classified information. Of special interest is any failure to provide truthful and candid answers during the security clearance process or any other failure to cooperate with the security clearance process.

The following will normally result in an unfavorable clearance action or administrative termination of further processing for clearance eligibility:

a) refusal, or failure without reasonable cause, to undergo or cooperate with security processing, including but not limited to meeting with a security investigator for subject interview, completing security forms or releases, and cooperation with medical or psychological evaluation;

b) refusal to provide full, frank, and truthful answers to lawful questions of investigators, security officials, or other official representatives in connection with a personnel security or trustworthiness determination.

Conditions that could raise a security concern and may be disqualifying include:

a) deliberate omission, concealment, or falsification of relevant facts from any personnel security questionnaire, personal history statement, or similar form used to conduct investigations, determine employment qualifications, award benefits or status, determine security clearance eligibility or trustworthiness, or award fiduciary responsibilities;

b) deliberately providing false or misleading information concerning relevant facts to an employer, investigator, security official, competent medical authority, or other official government representative;

c) credible adverse information in several adjudicative issue areas that is not sufficient for an adverse determination under any other single guideline, but which, when considered as a whole, supports a whole-person assessment of questionable judgment, untrustworthiness, unreliability, lack of candor, unwillingness to comply with rules and regulations, or other characteristics indicating that the person may not properly safeguard protected information;

d) credible adverse information that is not explicitly covered under any other guideline and may not be sufficient by itself for an adverse determination, but which, when combined with all available information, supports a whole-person assessment of questionable judgment, untrustworthiness, unreliability, lack of candor, unwillingness to comply with rules and regulations, or other characteristics indicating that the person may not properly safeguard protected information. This includes but is not limited to consideration of:

    1. untrustworthy or unreliable behavior to include breach of client confidentiality, release of proprietary information, unauthorized release of sensitive corporate or other government protected information;

    2. disruptive, violent, or other inappropriate behavior in the workplace;

    3. a pattern of dishonesty or rule violations;

    4. evidence of significant misuse of Government or other employer's time or resources;

e) personal conduct, or concealment of information about one's conduct, that creates a vulnerability to exploitation, manipulation, or duress, such as (1) engaging in activities which, if known, may affect the person's personal, profession, or community standing, or (2) while in another country, engaging in any activity that is illegal in that country or that is legal in that country but illegal in the United States and may serve as a basis for exploitation or pressure by the foreign security or intelligence service or other group;

f) violation of a written or recorded commitment made by the individual to the employer as a condition of employment;

g) association with persons involved in criminal activity.

Conditions that could mitigate security concerns include:

a) the individual made prompt, good-faith efforts to correct the omission, concealment, or falsification before being confronted with the facts;

b) the refusal or failure to cooperate, omission, or concealment was caused or significantly contributed to by improper or inadequate advice of authorized personnel or legal counsel advising or instructing the individual specifically concerning the security clearance process. Upon being made aware of the requirement to cooperate or provide the information, the individual cooperated fully and truthfully.

c) the offense is so minor, or so much time has passed, or the behavior is so infrequent, or it happened under such unique circumstances that it is unlikely to recur and does not cast doubt on the individual's reliability, trustworthiness, or good judgment;

d) the individual has acknowledged the behavior and obtained counseling to change the behavior or taken other positive steps to alleviate the stressors, circumstances, or factors that caused untrustworthy, unreliable, or other inappropriate behavior, and such behavior is unlikely to recur;

e) the individual has taken positive steps to reduce or eliminate vulnerability to exploitation, manipulation, or duress;

f) the information was unsubstantiated or from a source of questionable reliability;

g) association with persons involved in criminal activity has ceased or occurs under circumstances that do not cast doubt upon the individual's reliability, trustworthiness, judgment, or willingness to comply with rules and regulations.

This guideline is very often used to trip applicants up, and it is probably the primary one used to deny or revoke security clearances. Any time there is a concern expressed by the government under Guideline E, I am always on hyper alert since this can be a difficult one to overcome. Most often, the government will charge and express a concern under a different guideline but then add this one as a catch-all, using the same behavior that was expressed in the separate guideline(s). This is also the specific guideline that will be used if the government alleges that there was a deliberate omission, concealment, or falsification on the SF 86 or any type of similar investigation form. This is in addition to the catch-all nature of this guideline, which essentially says that the applicant has done all manner of other bad things, whether it is criminal activity, drugs, alcohol, or financial issues, to include failing to file tax returns. This guideline will then be thrown in as a kitchen sink approach. Again, there are ways to work around this one in mitigation, but it takes a Herculean effort to do so.

Guideline F: Financial Considerations

The Concern. Failure or inability to live within one's means, satisfy debts, and meet financial obligations may indicate poor self-control, lack of judgment, or unwillingness to abide by rules and regulations, all of which can raise questions about an individual's reliability, trustworthiness, and ability to protect classified information. An individual who is financially overextended is at risk of having to engage in illegal acts to generate funds. Compulsive gambling is a concern as it may lead to financial crimes, including espionage. Affluence that cannot be explained by known sources of income is also a security concern. It may indicate proceeds from financially profitable criminal acts.

Conditions that could raise a security concern and may be disqualifying include:

a) inability or unwillingness to satisfy debts;

b) indebtedness caused by frivolous or irresponsible spending and the absence of any evidence of willingness or intent to pay the debt or establish a realistic plan to pay the debt;

c) a history of not meeting financial obligations;

d) deceptive or illegal financial practices such as embezzlement, employee theft, check fraud, income tax evasion, expense account fraud, filing deceptive loan statements, and other intentional financial breaches of trust;

e) consistent spending beyond one's means, which may be indicated by excessive indebtedness, significant negative cash flow, high debt-to-income ratio, and/or financial analysis;

f) financial problems that are linked to drug abuse, alcoholism, gambling problems, or other issues or security concern;

g) failure to file annual Federal, state, or local income tax returns as required or the fraudulent filing of the same;

h) unexplained affluence, as shown by a lifestyle of standard of living, increase in net worth, or money transfers that cannot be explained by subject's known legal sources of income;

i) compulsive or addictive gambling as indicated by an unsuccessful attempt to stop gambling, "chasing losses" (i.e., increasing the bets or returning another day in an effort to get even), concealment of gambling losses, borrowing money to fund gambling debts, family conflict or other problems caused by gambling.

Conditions that could mitigate security concerns include:

a) the behavior happened so long ago, was so infrequent, or occurred under such circumstances that it is unlikely to recur and does not cast doubt on the individual's current reliability, trustworthiness, or good judgment;

b) the conditions that resulted in the financial problem were largely beyond the person's control (e.g., loss of employment, a business downturn, unexpected medical emergency, or a death, divorce, or separation), and the individual acted responsibly under the circumstances;

c) the person has received or is receiving counseling for the problem and/or there are clear indications that the problem is being resolved or is under control;

d) the individual initiated a good-faith effort to repay overdue creditors or otherwise resolve debts;

e) the individual has a reasonable basis to dispute the legitimacy of the past-due debt which is the cause of the problem and provided documented proof to substantiate the basis of the dispute or provides evidence of actions to resolve the issue;

f) the affluence resulted from a legal source of income.

This guideline would be considered the Big Kahuna as far as giving applicants and even people with clearances problems with their clearance applications. I have discussed this with a number of security clearance judges and government counsel and, in addition to my own experience, financial considerations make up a majority of the cases where clearances are suspended, revoked, or outright denied. The critical thing for people confronting financial issues is to make sure everything is currently being resolved. A person needs to have a plan to address any outstanding debts. He or she also needs to have a plan discussing how he or she got into the situation in the first place. Under the mitigation in this section, a bankruptcy is acceptable as legally allowed to "otherwise resolve debts." What I generally tell people who come to me with this area of concern is that more than one bankruptcy in their lifetime can pose a problem for them. If that is the case, I always like to see the second bankruptcy as being the chapter 13 debt consolidation type with a strong attempt to pay back all of the debt, oftentimes called a 100 percent plan. As soon as the bankruptcy is filed, regardless of what type, we suggest sending an email to the facility security officer along with a written explanation of the circumstances regarding the bankruptcy. Here is what those instructions and email look like:

Instructions:

I am writing this email to you after the signing of your bankruptcy petition. The bankruptcy petition will be filed with the bankruptcy court shortly. By copy of this email, your caseworker will email to you the entire filed petition. As we discussed, since you have a security clearance, we strongly advise you to immediately report the bankruptcy filing to your facility security officer (FSO). What we recommend is that you get the name and email address for your FSO. Once you have that and the PDF of the bankruptcy petition, then write an email to your FSO along the following lines:

Email:

(FSO name) - Since I hold a security clearance, I want to report to you that I have filed a bankruptcy petition. Please find attached a copy of the petition that was filed with the bankruptcy court. Again, since I am up front about everything as it relates to my clearance, I wanted to immediately get this information to you. Please let me know if you need any further information and I will get it to you right away. Thank you. (your name)

Follow-up instructions:

At the same time that you send this email to your FSO, prepare a separate document containing a paragraph or two that you write *to yourself* that explains how you got in this situation, the specific reasons why, how you think this will take care of it, and how you feel about the future. That way, you have a contemporaneous document to refer to if you get any questions from the Central Adjudications Facility (CAF) or JPAS regarding your security clearance. As an aside, our office also handles all types of issues as they relate to security clearances, so if you have questions or problems, please feel free to reach out to us. Thank you. www.SecurityClearanceDefenseLaywer.com

In simple terms, again, the debt must be addressed and dealt with in some form or fashion. The hardest cases I see are those that have outstanding debt and have made no attempt to resolve the debt. As an aside, and this also applies to Guideline E for personal conduct, make sure all of your tax returns are filed in a timely manner! It is a big problem if someone has not filed tax returns. That problem is then compounded by the fact that someone may owe back taxes. Make sure tax returns are always filed on time, and if you owe the IRS or any state taxing authority, work out a plan of repayment. Always have proof of whatever plan or resolution you reach with any creditor. It is also a very good idea to initially get your credit reports from annualcreditreport.com while you are getting ready to fill out the initial SF 86 so that you know exactly what the government is looking at with regard to your situation.

Here's information on how to go about doing that:

HOW CAN I GET MY FREE CREDIT REPORTS?

Pursuant to the Federal Trade Commission (FTC) rules, all individuals in the United States are entitled to one free credit report each year from each of the three credit reporting agencies, Equifax, Experian, and TransUnion. The **ONLY WAY** to get your actual, true free credit reports is from **www.annualcreditreport.com**

If you are contemplating a bankruptcy filing, it is, in our opinion, acceptable to get your credit reports directly from the website, **www.annualcreditreport.com Before** you go to this website, **PLEASE** make sure your computer is attached to a **working printer** and that you **PRINT** all pages of **ALL** of your credit reports as you will only be able to view them one time and you will NOT be able to visit the site again. **This is very important!**

If, however, you need credit reports for any other purpose and, most importantly, if you are contesting something you think should not be on your credit report, **DO NOT** get the credit reports online at this site. What you need to do is to get the mail-in form from **www.annual-creditreport.com** and fill it out and physically mail it in to the Atlanta address on the form itself. For credit report disputes, it is very important that you do not agree to any type of binding arbitration which may preclude you from filing a lawsuit if your credit reports are damaged through no fault of your own. As a result, it is advisable to get your credit reports this way only if you believe you will have to dispute your credit report. **As a general rule and as explained above, for bankruptcy purposes, getting all three credit reports online, again, is acceptable and is probably the quickest way for you to get them.** Please note that sometimes when you mail in the form for the request, you may be told by that website that it cannot verify that you are who you say you are. As a result, when you mail the form in, you may want to include a utility bill or a phone bill or some type of bill that ties you to the address where you state that you reside. This is where the credit reports will be mailed.

One last thing in this area that is important. If you dispute any debt or anything that appears to be erroneous on your credit report, please make sure all disputes and issues that you see with either a debt collector or on your credit report, are addressed in writing, by certified mail, return receipt requested. Please also keep a copy of every dispute or issue you have, in writing, so that you can use that as an attachment when filling out the SF 86, which then bolsters your explanation about the dispute or problem.

Guideline G: Alcohol Consumption

The Concern. Excessive alcohol consumption often leads to the exercise of questionable judgment or the failure to control impulses, and can raise questions about an individual's reliability and trustworthiness.

Conditions that could raise a security concern and may be disqualifying include:

a) alcohol-related incidents away from work, such as driving while under the influence, fighting, child or spouse abuse, disturbing the peace, or other incidents of concern, regardless of whether the individual is diagnosed as an alcohol abuser or alcohol dependent;

b) alcohol-related incidents at work, such as reporting for work or duty in an intoxicated or impaired condition, or drinking on the job, regardless of whether the individual is diagnosed as an alcohol abuser or alcohol dependent;

c) habitual or binge consumption of alcohol to the point of impaired judgment, regardless of whether the individual is diagnosed as an alcohol abuser or alcohol dependent;

d) diagnosis by a duly qualified medical professional (e.g., physician, clinical psychologist, or psychiatrist) of alcohol abuse or alcohol dependence;

e) evaluation of alcohol abuse or alcohol dependence by a licensed clinical social worker who is a staff member of a recognized alcohol treatment program;

f) relapse after diagnosis of alcohol abuse or dependence and completion of an alcohol rehabilitation program;

g) failure to follow any court order regarding alcohol education, evaluation, treatment, or abstinence.

Conditions that could mitigate security concerns include:

a) so much time has passed, or the behavior was so infrequent, or it happened under such unusual circumstances that it is unlikely to recur or does not cast doubt on the individual's current reliability, trustworthiness, or good judgment;

b) the individual acknowledges his or her alcoholism or issues of alcohol abuse, provides evidence of actions taken to overcome this problem, and has established a pattern of abstinence (if alcohol dependent) or responsible use (if an alcohol abuser);

    c)   the individual is a current employee who is participating in a counseling or treatment program, has no history of previous treatment and relapse, and is making satisfactory progress;

    d)   the individual has successfully completed inpatient or outpatient counseling or rehabilitation along with any required aftercare, has demonstrated a clear and established pattern of modified consumption or abstinence in accordance with treatment recommendations, such as participation in meetings of Alcoholics Anonymous or a similar organization and has received a favorable prognosis by a duly qualified medical professional or a licensed clinical social worker who is a staff member of a recognized alcohol treatment program.

As I have mentioned before, alcohol consumption is one of the top three reasons that people either lose their security clearances or have them denied in the first place. If I had to place these issues in rank order, it is usually financial concerns, alcohol consumption, and then drug involvement. Obviously, a large proportion of our society has, unfortunately, issues with alcohol. When the government raises this concern, it allows for mitigation regarding alcohol usage. The critical components to look to for mitigation are that so much time is passed from the usage or, that the behavior was so infrequent, that it is unlikely to recur and does not cast doubt on the individual's current reliability, trustworthiness, or good judgment. Beyond that, and what I think would be very critical to a favorable clearance decision, is that the individual acknowledges his or her alcoholism or issues of alcohol abuse, provides evidence of actions taken to overcome this problem, and establishes a pattern of abstinence if alcohol dependent or responsible use if alcohol abuser. Additionally, and this is ever so important, the government likes to see successful completion of inpatient or outpatient counseling and rehabilitation along with any required aftercare and the applicant has demonstrated a clear and established pattern of modified consumption or absence in accordance with treatment recommendations, such as participations in meetings of Alcoholics Anonymous or similar organizations. To this point, and I cannot overstate it, if someone has an issue with alcohol, or if the government alleges that someone has an issue with alcohol, I absolutely recommend immediate and sustained attendance in AA. I recommend this to every client who receives a guideline G alcohol consumption statement of reasons to revoke a security clearance. Probably half the time, I will have people tell me that they don't really need to go to AA and that they don't really have a problem with alcohol. If you want to keep your clearance, please follow this advice. The worst thing that happens with someone going to AA during the entire duration of concerns about the security clearance is that you won't drink, you miss a little bit of time in your week, maybe 3 to 5 times per week where you go to an AA meeting and do some introspection and a personal self-check. As an aside, you will save money since you will not be out drinking or partying or whatever it is you are considering doing. I see nothing but good coming out of this and no bad side effects. Of course, the overarching positive aspect will be that this will put you in the best possible chance to retain a clearance if the government has stated it has concerns about your access to classified material in light of your alcohol consumption. If the phrase alcohol consumption and security clearance is ever used with regard to your security clearance, PLEASE, PLEASE, PLEASE attend AA, at a minimum, during the entire time that this concern has been raised and it will do you a world of good!

Guideline H: Drug Involvement

The Concern. Use of an illegal drug or misuse of a prescription drug can raise questions about an individual's reliability and trustworthiness, both because it may impair judgment, and because it raises questions about a person's ability or willingness to comply with laws, rules, and regulations.

a) Drugs are defined as mood and behavior altering substances, and include:

   1. Drugs, materials, and other chemical compounds identified and listed in the Controlled Substances Act of 1970, as amended (e.g., marijuana or cannabis, depressants, narcotics, stimulants, and hallucinogens), and

   2. inhalants and other similar substances:

b) drug abuse is the illegal use of a drug or use of a legal drug in a manner that deviates from approved medical direction.

Conditions that could raise a security concern and may be disqualifying include:

a) any drug abuse (see above definition);[2]

b) testing positive for illegal drug use;

c) illegal drug possession, including cultivation, processing, manufacture, purchase, sale, or distribution; or possession of drug paraphernalia;

d) diagnosis by a duly qualified medical professional (e.g., physician, clinical psychologist, or psychiatrist) of drug abuse or drug dependence;

e) evaluation of drug abuse or drug dependence by a licensed clinical social worker who is a staff member of a recognized drug treatment program;

f) failure to successfully complete a drug treatment program prescribed by a duly qualified medical professional;

g) any illegal drug use after being granted a security clearance;

h) expressed intent to continue illegal drug use, or failure to clearly and convincingly commit to discontinue drug use.

[2] Under the provisions of 10 U.S.C. 986 any person who is an unlawful user of, or is addicted to, a controlled substance as defined in section 102 of the Controlled Substances Act (21 U.S.C. 802), may not be granted or have renewed their access to classified information.

Conditions that could mitigate security concerns include:

a) the behavior happened so long ago, was so infrequent, or happened under such circumstances that it is unlikely to recur or does not cast doubt on the individual's current reliability, trustworthiness, or good judgment;

b) a demonstrated intent not to abuse any drugs in the future, such as:

    1. disassociation from drug-using associates and contacts;

    2. changing or avoiding the environment where drugs were used;

    3. an appropriate period of abstinence;

    4. a signed statement of intent with automatic revocation of clearance for any violation;

c) abuse of prescription drugs was after a severe or prolonged illness during which these drugs were prescribed, and abuse has since ended;

d) satisfactory completion of a prescribed drug treatment program, including, but not limited to, rehabilitation and aftercare requirements, without recurrence of abuse, and a favorable prognosis by a duly qualified medical professional.

This guideline falls under the last of what I call the big three, as far as the government's major concerns regarding somebody's access to classified material. There are several avenues of mitigation for drug involvement. The problem, of course, comes under, as we shall see, Guideline J, criminal conduct. A person for whom drugs have been an issue was, in all likelihood, using the drugs illegally, so the government will usually add the charge of Guideline J, criminal conduct, as well. It is important to show that the behavior happened long ago, was infrequent, or happened under such circumstances that it is unlikely to recur and does not cast doubt on an individual's current reliability, trustworthiness, or good judgment. A security clearance applicant also has to show a demonstrated intent not to abuse any illegal drugs in the future such as disassociation from drug-using associates and contacts, changing the social environment where drugs are used, an appropriate period of abstinence, and a signed statement of intent with automatic revocation of the clearance for any violation in the future. There is also a mitigation provision and an allowance if there was an abuse of prescription drugs after a severe or prolonged illness during which these drugs were prescribed and the abuse has since ended.

Finally, there is a catchall provision of satisfactory completion of a prescribed drug treatment program, including but not limited to rehabilitation and aftercare requirements, without recurrence of abuse, and a favorable prognosis by a duly qualified medical professional. If I ever have a case where drug involvement is the issue, I don't care how long ago it happened—I strongly recommend rehab and, at a minimum, a strong commitment to an AA or NA type of program. AA can cover a lot of ground and everyone knows what it is. As stated above, attendance certainly won't hurt somebody who has had a prior addiction problem!

Guideline I: Psychological Conditions

The Concern. Certain emotional, mental, and personality conditions can impair judgment, reliability, or trustworthiness. A formal diagnosis of a disorder is not required for there to be a concern under this guideline. A duly qualified mental health professional (e.g., clinical psychologist or psychiatrist) employed by, or acceptable to and approved by the U.S. Government, should be consulted when evaluating potentially disqualifying and mitigating information under this guideline. No negative inference concerning the standards in this guideline may be raised solely on the basis of seeking mental health counseling.

Conditions that could raise a security concern and may be disqualifying include:

   a)   behavior that casts doubt on an individual's judgment, reliability, or trustworthiness that is not covered under any other guideline, including but not limited to emotionally unstable, irresponsible, dysfunctional, violent, paranoid, or bizarre behavior;

b)   an opinion by a duly qualified mental health professional that the individual has a condition not covered under any other guideline that may impair judgment, reliability, or trustworthiness;[3]

c)   the individual has failed to follow treatment advice related to a diagnosed emotional, mental, or personality condition, e.g., failure to take prescribed medication.

Conditions that could mitigate security concerns include:

a)   the identified condition is readily controllable with treatment, and the individual has demonstrated ongoing and consistent compliance with the treatment plan;

b)   the individual has voluntarily entered a counseling or treatment program for a condition that is amenable to treatment, and the individual is currently receiving counseling or treatment with a favorable prognosis by a duly qualified mental health professional;

c)   recent opinion by a duly qualified mental health professional employed by, or acceptable to and approved by the U.S. Government that an individual's previous condition is under control or in remission, and has a low probability of recurrence or exacerbation;

d)   the past emotional instability was a temporary condition (e.g., one caused by death, illness, or marital breakup), the situation has been resolved, and the individual no longer shows indications of emotional instability;

e)   there is no indication of a current problem.

---

[3] Under the provisions of 10 U.S.C. 986, a person who is mentally incompetent, as determined by a credentialed mental health professional approved by the Department of Defense, may not be granted or have renewed their access to classified information.

At the outset, it is important to note that the directive itself under this guideline states that "no negative inference concerning the standards in this guideline may be raised solely on the basis of seeking mental health counseling." The point is that people who hold security clearances or applicants for the same are allowed to seek out assistance from mental health professionals. Of course, as we have previously reviewed the SF 86, the questions regarding mental health counseling must be answered exactly. If the government raises an issue or concern regarding a security clearance under Guideline I, then there are conditions that are allowed to be shown that will mitigate security clearance concerns. These conditions include showing that the problem is readily controllable with treatment and that the individual has demonstrated ongoing and consistent compliance with the treatment plan. Also, there is an allowance for an individual who has voluntarily entered counseling or a treatment program for a condition that is amenable to treatment, and the individual is currently receiving counseling or treatment, with a favorable prognosis offered by a duly qualified mental health professional. An applicant can also show a recent opinion by a duly qualified mental health professional employed by or acceptable to the government that an individual's previous condition is under control or in remission, and the individual has a low probability of recurrence or exacerbation. There is also a provision where an applicant can show that the past emotional instability was a temporary condition, for example caused by death, illness or marital breakup, the situation has been resolved, and the individual no longer shows indications of emotional instability. And, finally, one can show that there is no indication of a current problem. The point here is that it is possible to work around government concerns as they relate to psychological conditions. Ongoing treatment and a positive prognosis are, as a general rule, the keys here.

Guideline J: Criminal Conduct

The Concern. Criminal activity creates doubt about a person's judgment, reliability, and trustworthiness. By its very nature, it calls into question a person's ability or willingness to comply with laws, rules, and regulations.

Conditions that could raise a security concern and may be disqualifying include:

a) a single serious crime or multiple lesser offenses;

b) discharge or dismissal from the Armed Forces under dishonorable conditions;[4]

c) allegation or admission of criminal conduct, regardless of whether the person was formally charged, formally prosecuted, or convicted;

d) individual is currently on parole or probation;

e) violation of parole or probation, or failure to complete a court-mandated rehabilitation program;

f) conviction in a Federal or State court, including a court-martial of a crime, sentenced to imprisonment for a term exceeding one year and incarcerated as a result of that sentence for not less than a year.[5]

Conditions that could mitigate security concerns include:

a) so much time has elapsed since the criminal behavior happened, or it happened under such unusual circumstances, that it is unlikely to recur and does not cast doubt on the individual's reliability, trustworthiness, or good judgment;

---

[4] Under the provisions of 10 U.S.C. 986, a person who has received a dishonorable discharge or has been dismissed from the Armed Forces may not be granted or have renewed access to classified information. In a meritorious case, the Secretaries of the Military Departments or designee, or the Directors of WH, DIA, NSA, DOHA or designee may authorize a waiver of this prohibition. Waiver authority may not be further delegated to a member of the Component Personnel Security Appeal Board or the DOHA Security Clearance Appeal Board.

[5] Under the above-mentioned statute, a person who has been convicted in a Federal or State court, including court-martials, sentenced to imprisonment for a term exceeding one year and incarcerated for not less than one year, may not be granted or have renewed access to classified information. The same waiver provision also applies.

b) the person was pressured or coerced into committing the act and those pressures are no longer present in the person's life;

c) there is evidence that the person did not commit the offense;

d) there is evidence of successful rehabilitation, including but not limited to the passage of time without recurrence of criminal activity, remorse or restitution, job training or higher education, good employment record, or constructive community involvement;

e) potentially disqualifying conditions (b) and (f) above may not be mitigated unless, where meritorious circumstances exist, the Secretaries of the Military Departments or designee; or the Directors of Washington Headquarters Services (WHS), Defense Intelligence Agency (DIA), National Security Agency (NSA), Defense Office of Hearings and Appeals (DOHA) or designee, has granted a waiver.

Criminal conduct is one of the toughest areas of government concern for security clearance holders and applicants to work through. It is not insurmountable, however, and is usually accompanied with underlying problematic behavior such as drug involvement, DUIs, domestic violence charges, etc. As a result, I always advise applicants to focus on the underlying issues if addressed accordingly on a statement of reasons issued by the government, and that will give you the ammunition needed to address the criminal conduct. As far as mitigation is concerned, a person can show that so much time has elapsed since the criminal behavior happened or it happened under such unusual circumstances that it is unlikely to recur and does not cast doubt on the individual's reliability, trustworthiness, and good judgment. A person can also show that he or she was pressured or coerced into committing the acts, and the temptations and pressures are no longer present in the person's life. A person can also show that there is evidence of successful rehabilitation, including but not limited to the passage of time without recurrence of criminal activity, remorse or restitution, job training or higher education, good employment record, or constructive community involvement.

Guideline K: Handling Protected Information

The Concern. Deliberate or negligent failure to comply with rules and regulations for protecting classified or other sensitive information raises doubt about an individual's trustworthiness, judgment, reliability, or willingness and ability to safeguard such information, and is a serious security concern.

Conditions that could raise a security concern and may be disqualifying include:

a) deliberate or negligent disclosure of classified or other protected information to unauthorized persons, including but not limited to personal or business contacts, to the media, or to persons present at seminars, meetings, or conferences;

b) collecting or storing classified or other protected information at home or in any other unauthorized location;

c) loading, drafting, editing, modifying, storing, transmitting, or otherwise handling classified reports, data, or other information on any unapproved equipment including but not limited to any typewriter, word processor, or computer hardware, software, drive, system, gameboard, handheld, "palm" or pocket device or other adjunct equipment;

d) inappropriate efforts to obtain or view classified or other protected information outside one's need to know;

e) copying classified or other protected information in a manner designed to conceal or remove classification or other document control markings;

f) viewing or downloading information from a secure system when the information is beyond the individual's need-to-know;

g) any failure to comply with rules for the protection of classified or other sensitive information;

h) negligence or lax security habits that persist despite counseling by management.

i) failure to comply with rules or regulations that results in damage to the National Security, regardless of whether it was deliberate or negligent.

Conditions that could mitigate security concerns include:

a) so much time has elapsed since the behavior, or it has happened so infrequently or under such unusual circumstances, that it is unlikely to recur and does not cast doubt on the individual's current reliability, trustworthiness, or good judgment;

b) the individual responded favorably to counseling or remedial security training and now demonstrates a positive attitude toward the discharge of security responsibilities;

c) the security violations were due to improper or inadequate training.

Under the cases that I have handled under this guideline, I have found it fairly easy to show the mitigating factor that the behavior happened so infrequently or under such unusual circumstances, it is unlikely to recur. This stands to reason because if security violations are frequent and deliberate, then there is a tougher problem to confront. One can also show that the person responded favorably to counseling and demonstrates a positive attitude toward the discharge of security responsibilities. As long as someone is earnest, somber, and serious about handling protected information, it is usually not too difficult to successfully work through this government concern.

Guideline L: Outside Activities

The Concern. Involvement in certain types of outside employment or activities is of security concern if it poses a conflict of interest with an individual's security responsibilities and could create an increased risk of unauthorized disclosure of classified information.

Conditions that could raise a security concern and may be disqualifying include:

a) any employment or service, whether compensated or volunteer, with:

   1. the government of a foreign country;

   2. any foreign national, organization, or other entity;

   3. a representative of any foreign interest;

   4. any foreign, domestic, or international organization or person engaged in analysis, discussion, or publication of material on intelligence, defense, foreign affairs, or protected technology;

b) failure to report or fully disclose an outside activity when this is required.

Conditions that could mitigate security concerns include:

a) evaluation of the outside employment or activity by the appropriate security or counterintelligence office indicates that it does not pose a conflict with an individual's security responsibilities or with the national security interests of the United States;

b) the individual terminated the employment or discontinued the activity upon being notified that it was in conflict with his or her security responsibilities.

When there is an allegation under this guideline, it usually revolves around Guideline B, foreign influence, and Guideline C, foreign preference. As long as someone can mitigate the government's concerns under those two respective guidelines, he or she should be able to use the mitigation under Guideline L to work through these potential issues.

Guideline M: Use of Information Technology Systems

The Concern. Noncompliance with rules, procedures, guidelines, or regulations pertaining to information technology systems may raise security concerns about an individual's reliability and trustworthiness, calling into question the willingness or ability to properly protect sensitive systems, networks, and information.

Information technology systems include all related computer hardware, software, firmware, and data used for the communication, transmission, processing, manipulation, storage, or protection of information.

Conditions that could raise a security concern and may be disqualifying include:

a) illegal or unauthorized entry into any information technology system or component thereof;

b) illegal or unauthorized modification, destruction, manipulation, or denial of access to information, software, firmware, or hardware in an information technology system;

c) use of any information technology system to gain unauthorized access to another system or to a compartmented area within the same system;

d) downloading, storing, or transmitting classified information on or to any unauthorized software, hardware, or information technology system;

e) unauthorized use of a government or other information technology system;

f) introduction, removal, or duplication of hardware, firmware, software, or media to or from any information technology system without authorization, when prohibited by rules, procedures, guidelines, or regulations;

g) negligence or lax security habits in handling information technology that persist despite counseling by management,

h)   any misuse of information technology, whether deliberate or negligent, that results in damage to the national security.

Conditions that could mitigate security concerns include:

a)   so much time has elapsed since the behavior happened, or it happened under such unusual circumstances, that it is unlikely to recur and does not cast doubt on the individual's reliability, trustworthiness, or good judgment;

b)   the misuse was minor and done only in the interest of organizational efficiency and effectiveness, such as letting another person use one's password or computer when no other timely alternative was readily available;

c)   the conduct was unintentional or inadvertent and was followed by a prompt, good-faith effort to correct the situation and by notification of supervisor.

Surprisingly, I have seen and handled a number of cases under this guideline.

One wouldn't think that would be the case when issues arise with regard to use of information technology systems. But the critical mitigation to focus on is that the behavior almost always happens under such unusual circumstances that one can then show it is unlikely to recur and does not cast doubt on the individual's reliability, trustworthiness, or good judgment. Also, it is important to show that the misuse was minor and done only in the interest of organizational efficiency and effectiveness. Those are the areas where it is really important to mitigate the government's concerns. Of course, if the behavior was unintentional or inadvertent, then that is usually easy to work through as well.

CHAPTER 6

The Procedure (or What Happens Next)

The good news is that the vast majority of people who initially submit an application for a security clearance at the outset of their career—or those who already hold a security clearance—will never have to worry about a clearance being denied or revoked, and they will never have to be bothered to learn these clearance regulations. The issues only come about when the government cannot affirmatively find that it is clearly consistent with the national interest to grant or continue a security clearance for an applicant. In those situations, the guidelines require that the case be referred to DOHA (Department of Hearings and Appeals). Upon referral, the DOHA is required to make a prompt determination as to whether to grant or continue a security clearance, issue a statement of reasons (SOR) as to why it is not clearly consistent with the national interest to do so, or take interim actions, including but not limited to the following:

a. Direct further investigation;

b. Propound written interrogatories to the applicant or other persons with relevant information;

c. Require the applicant to undergo a medical evaluation by a DOD psychiatric consultant;

d. Interview the applicant.

The procedural guidelines require that an unfavorable clearance decision shall not be made unless the applicant has been provided with a written Statement of Reason (SOR) that shall be as detailed and comprehensive as the national security permits. A letter of instruction with the SOR shall explain that the applicant or government department counsel may request a hearing. It shall also explain the adverse consequences for failure to respond to the SOR within the prescribed time frame.

The procedure requires that the applicant must submit a detailed written answer to the SOR under oath or affirmation that shall admit or deny each listed allegation. A general denial or other similar answer is insufficient. To be entitled to a hearing, the applicant must specifically request a hearing in his or her answer. The answer must be received by the DOHA within twenty days from receipt of the SOR.

If the applicant does not file a timely and responsive answer to the SOR, then the government may discontinue processing the case, deny issuance of the requested security clearance, and revoke any security clearance currently held by the applicant. On the other hand, should review of the applicant's answer to the SOR indicate that the allegations are unfounded, or that the evidence is insufficient for further processing, then the department counsel shall take such action as is appropriate under the circumstances, including, but not limited to, the withdrawal of the SOR.

If the applicant has not requested a hearing with his or her answer to the SOR and department counsel and has not requested a hearing within twenty days of receipt of the applicant's answer, the case shall be assigned to the administrative judge for a clearance decision based on the written record. Department counsel shall provide the applicant with a copy of all relevant and material information that could be introduced at a hearing. The applicant shall have thirty days from receipt of the information in which to submit a document to serve as a response setting forth objections, rebuttal, extenuation, mitigation, or explanation, as appropriate.

If a hearing is requested by the applicant or department counsel, the case shall be assigned to the administrative judge for a clearance decision based on the hearing record. Following issuance of a notice of hearing by the administrative judge, the applicant shall appear in person with or without counsel or personal representative at a time and place designated by the notice of hearing. The applicant shall have a reasonable amount of time to prepare his or her case. The applicant shall be notified at least fifteen days in advance of the time and place of the hearing, which generally shall be held at a location in the United States within a metropolitan area near the applicant's place of employment or residence. A continuance may be granted by the administrative judge only for good cause. Hearings may be held outside of the United States and NATO cases, or in other locations upon a finding of good cause.

The Administrative Judge (ALJ) may require a pre-hearing conference. The ALJ may rule on questions of procedure, discovery, and evidence and shall conduct all proceedings in a fair, timely, and orderly manner.

Discovery by the applicant is limited to non-privileged documents and the materials that are subject to control by the DOHA. Discovery by department counsel after issuance of an SOR may be granted by the ALJ only upon a showing of good cause.

The directive provides that the hearing is an open hearing, except when the applicant requests that it be closed or the ALJ determines that there is a need to protect classified information or other good cause. There is no negative inference as to the merits of the case on the basis of a request that the hearing be closed. Additionally, the government's lawyer, department counsel, and the applicant shall serve one another with a copy of any pleading, proposed documentary evidence, and any other written communication to be submitted to the ALJ. The government's lawyer, or department counsel, is responsible for presenting witnesses and other evidence to establish facts alleged in the SOR that have been contested. On the other hand, the applicant is responsible for presenting witnesses and other evidence to rebut, explain, extenuate, or mitigate facts admitted by applicant or proven by department counsel, and has the ultimate burden of persuasion as to obtaining a favorable clearance decision. Any witnesses that are called by either party are subject to cross-examination. Additionally, the SOR may be amended at the hearing by the ALJ on his or her own motion, upon motion by department counsel or the applicant, so as to render it in conformity with the evidence admitted or for other good cause. When such amendments are made, the ALJ may grant either party's request for such additional time as the judge may deem appropriate for further preparation or other good cause.

The ALJ shall notify the applicant and all witnesses who testify at the hearing that 18 U.S.C. 1001 is applicable. Importantly, the federal rules of evidence shall serve as a guide at the hearing. Relevant and material evidence may be received subject to rebuttal, and technical rules of evidence may be relaxed to permit the development of a full and complete record. Official records or evidence compiled and created in the regular course of business may be received and considered by the judge without authenticating witnesses, provided that such information has been furnished by an investigative agency.

A verbatim transcript shall be made of the hearing. The applicant is furnished one copy of the transcript, less the exhibits, without cost. Following the hearing, the ALJ shall make a written clearance decision in a timely manner setting forth pertinent findings of fact, policies, and conclusions as to the allegations in the SOR and whether it is clearly consistent with the national interest to grant or continue a security clearance for the applicant. Both the applicant and the department counsel will each be provided a copy of clearance decision. If the ALJ decides it is clearly consistent with the national interest for the applicant to be granted or to retain a security clearance, the government agencies will be notified when the clearance decision becomes final. On the other hand, if the ALJ decides that it is not clearly not consistent with the national interest for the applicant to be granted or to retain a security clearance, the government shall promptly notify the applicant's employer of the denial or revocation of the applicant security clearance. A letter forwarding the judge's clearance decision to the applicant shall advise the applicant of the actions taken and also advise the applicant that he or she may appeal the judge's clearance decision.

CHAPTER 7

Appeal of an Adverse ALJ Decision That Revokes or Denies a Security Clearance

Before we get into the appeal discussion, just a side note here. It has been my experience that it is absolutely critical to win a security clearance revocation or denial case at the ALJ level, which was described previously. That is the best opportunity to present a good, cogent case as to why a clearance should be granted or retained, and it is the absolute best shot an applicant will have. Suffice it to say, appeals beyond this level are awfully tough to win. Just to reiterate:

DO EVERYTHING in your power to win your case at the ALJ level or earlier!

The directive allows the applicant or the department counsel to appeal the ALJ's decision by filing a written notice of appeal with the Appeal Board within fifteen days after the date of the ALJ clearance decision. A notice of appeal received **after** fifteen days from the date of the clearance decision shall not be accepted by the Appeal Board. Upon receipt of a notice of appeal, the Appeal Board shall be provided the case record. No new evidence shall be received or considered by the Appeal Board.

After filing a timely notice of appeal, a written appeal brief must be received by the Appeal Board within forty-five days from the date of the ALJ clearance decision. The appeal brief must state the specific issue or issues being raised, and cite specific portions of the case record supporting any alleged error. A written reply brief, if any, must be filed within twenty days from receipt of the appeal brief. A copy of any brief must be served to the other side.

The appeal board addresses the material decisions raised by the parties to determine whether harmful error occurred. The scope of review for the Appeal Board is to determine whether the ALJ's findings of fact are supported by such relevant evidence as a reasonable mind might accept as adequate to support a conclusion in light of all the contrary evidence in the same record. In making the review, the Appeal Board gives deference to the credibility determinations by the ALJ and views whether the judge adhered to the procedures required or whether the judge's rulings or conclusions were arbitrary, capricious, or contrary to law. The Appeal Board then issues a written clearance decision addressing the material issues raised on appeal. The Appeal Board has the authority to affirm the decision of the ALJ or to remand the case to an ALJ to correct identified errors. If the case is remanded, the Appeal Board shall specify the action to be taken on remand or reverse the decision of the ALJ if correction of identified errors mandates such action. A copy of the Appeal Board's written decision is to be provided to all of the parties.

A clearance decision is considered final upon the following circumstances: 1. A security clearance is granted or continued; 2. No timely notice of appeal is filed; 3. No timely appeal brief is filed after a notice of appeal has been filed; 4. The appeal has been withdrawn; 5. The appeal board affirms or reverses the ALJ clearance decision; or 6. When a decision has been made by the Secretary of Defense or the department or agency head responsible.

An applicant whose security clearance has finally been denied or revoked by the DOHA is barred from reapplication for one year from the date of the initial unfavorable clearance decision. A reapplication for a security clearance must be made initially by the applicant's employer and is subject to the same processing requirements as those for a new security clearance application. As a result, this one-year period gives ample time for a prospective applicant to try to mitigate the concerns expressed by the government from the previous denial or revocation of the security clearance.

CHAPTER 8

How a Clearance Case Should be Handled
When the Government Is Intent on Denying
or Revoking a Clearance

The information in this chapter is *my personal view* on how to handle a case where a security clearance is in jeopardy either from being revoked by the government or a denial. Of course, this section is based upon my own experience. I am painfully aware that when people run into clearance problems and their very livelihood is in jeopardy, they are most often in a panicked state, and rightfully so.

These bullet points/ideas represent how I think someone should approach a clearance revocation or denial. Of course, the earlier someone gets out in front of this problem or any type of clearance issue, the better. It's wise to get counsel as early as possible, starting with troubling or problematic questions on the SF 86 through any interrogatories and/or interviews and polygraph examinations through the hearing stage, if it has to get that far. To take this one step further, if anything at all happens to someone who holds an active security clearance, it is probably advisable to get counsel at that point so the person can begin to take affirmative steps to safeguard the clearance, no matter what the current situation entails.

In my experience, wherever government and government contracting work is done, approximately 65 percent of all work done by the government employees and private contractors is now classified. What that means, in a nutshell, is that in order to work on any classified material, you need a security clearance for access to that material. This figure of 65 percent is just based on my experience, but the disturbing part of that equation is that it was probably only 30 percent ten years ago and maybe 50 percent five years ago. In a nutshell, I see that more of the government work will require access to classified material in the future and not less. In fact, many employers now require someone to already have a secret or top-secret security clearance before they are even hired since it is taking so long just to get an interim clearance.

A. Evaluation of a Case from My Perspective

1. How a case starts

    a. Someone has a clearance or applies for a clearance and receives from a security office a Statement of Reasons (SOR) from the government stating an intent to revoke or not give a clearance.

    b. The SOR will give the specific reasons why the clearance is intended to be revoked or denied.

    c. It will state the specific reasons under DOD Directive 5220.6 for the revocation or denial.

    d. It will give an opportunity to submit a rebuttal statement.

    e. It will give an opportunity to request a hearing before an administrative law judge (ALJ).

2. Applicant's choices:

    a. Two ways to approach this

        i. Defending a case simply on paper

        ii. Submitting a rebuttal statement only

    b. Requesting a hearing before an ALJ

        i. Hearing before an ALJ is an adversarial proceeding.

        ii. Both parties, government and applicant, have a responsibility to present their respective cases.

iii. Government is normally represented by an attorney known as department counsel.

iv. Applicant has option of appearing by himself/herself, being represented by an attorney selected and paid for by the applicant, or being represented by a personal representative such as a friend or family member.

v. Hearing before ALJ is conducted in a locality within 150 miles of the residence or place of employment of the applicant.

vi. An ALJ is not empowered to issue a subpoena and, as a result, appearance of witnesses or production of documents is purely voluntary.

vii. Counsel must submit a notice of appearance with Department Counsel and Hearing Office.

viii. Parties have a wide degree of discretion in order to present the evidence in their cases.

ix. Federal rules of evidence are used as a guide.

x. All witnesses are subject to cross examination by the other party.

B. **My View of a Case**

1. **ALWAYS** request a hearing! I cannot stress this approach in any stronger terms!

2. Submitting a rebuttal statement and NOT requesting a hearing before an administrative judge is a waste of time.

3. Applicant is not responsible for the conduct:

   a. Fight it as you would any defense-postured case.

4. Applicant is responsible for the conduct:

   a. Explain conduct – Note that I have NEVER handled a hearing where the applicant wasn't responsible for the conduct. Recall that the rules of evidence do not apply, so whatever the government alleges has happened in the past in all likelihood has happened. The benefit is to use mitigation to explain and water down the conduct in order to alleviate the government's concerns about the applicant's access to classified material.

    b.   Mitigating circumstances

5.   Steps if applicant is responsible for the conduct.

    a.   Explain the conduct in great detail.

    b.   In my cases, the applicant will testify.

    c.   Bring in supporting witnesses.

    d.   Character witnesses

    e.   Conduct witnesses where applicable—i.e., drugs, alcohol, financial—to help explain a change or improvement in behavior.

    f.   Produce and present written documentation.

    g.   Awards

    h.   Diplomas

    i.   Produce and present employment history documentation.

    j.   Produce and present officer efficiency reports (OERs) and enlisted efficiency reports (EERs) if prior military. Also, if prior military, submit an SF 180, which is available online, to get your entire military file.

    k.   Guidelines for Determining Eligibility for Access to Classified Information.

    l.   Each guideline that states an intent to revoke a security clearance has mitigating guidelines.

m. Even if the applicant is found guilty of the conduct, the mitigating circumstances could still allow them to minimize the concern for a security risk.

n. We have previously covered all the mitigation that is allowed and available under the directive for each guideline. For each guideline referenced in the SOR, make sure it is explained away in the hearing with written documents and testimony in great detail.

6. Appeal process from an adverse decision by an ALJ.

a. The issue is whether it is clearly consistent with the national interest to grant an applicant a security clearance for access to classified, secret, or top secret information.

b. Favorable – clearance

c. Unfavorable – no clearance

d. Written notice of appeal with Appeal Board within fifteen days of the date of the ALJ decision/applicant or government through department counsel

e. No new evidence shall be received or considered by the Appeal Board.

f. A written appeal brief must be received by the Appeal Board within forty-five days from the date of the ALJ's clearance decision.

g. Must state specific issues being raised and site specific portions of the case record supporting an alleged error.

h. Appeal Board looks at whether the ALJ adhered to procedures; whether rulings or conclusions were arbitrary, capricious, or contrary to law.

Get out in front of any and all security clearance concerns as absolutely early as possible. Practice and rewrite your answers to make sure they are perfect and relevant to any and all questions that give you even the slightest bit of concern BEFORE you submit the SF 86. Have someone review your proposed answers and re-work them until they are perfect BEFORE you submit the SF 86. Make sure the SF 86 is answered fully, completely, and honestly. More detail is better than less!

Do NOT EVER make a misstatement or omission on the SF 86! That is almost always worse than ANY problematic behavior or history that you do disclose. The toughest cases to defend against are those where the government has alleged an intentional misstatement under Guideline E.

If the government submits written interrogatories to you about any answers on the SF 86, it may be trying to dig into your past. Like the answers to the SF 86, make sure that the answers you give to any written interrogatories are practiced, reviewed, and perfect BEFORE you submit them to the government.

When you have to give an interview to a government investigator or undergo a polygraph examination, my theory is this: your story is what your story has always been as previously presented to the government. In my experience, if you change anything during an interviewer polygraph examination from what you put down on the SF 86, that will be a huge problem, which is why it is so important to get out in front of this early and stay consistent with the story of your history throughout the process.

If the government issues an SOR to either deny or revoke a security clearance, remember that it is possible to prevail despite what seem to be dire circumstances. If an SOR is issued, make sure that you:

A.   Always request a hearing.

B.   Bring a case as big as possible.

C.   Have a third party represent you. It is a lot easier for a third party to say what a great person you are and talk about your wonderful background and all of the good work you do in the great life that you have led versus you saying that yourself. It is no different than that old adage, "A lawyer who represents himself has a fool for a client." You don't even need a lawyer; you can have any third party represent you.

As I mentioned, I take this work very seriously. I know how important it is to get a good-paying job where a security clearance is required, not only for financial security, but also for meaningful work. Please feel free to contact me at rsykstus@bondnbotes or by phone at 256-713-0221 if you need assistance.

CHAPTER 9

New Directive

This is an urgent chapter that I have just added. As this book was shipped off to the publisher, it was announced that a new directive has been issued by the government for security clearance cases. As a result, PLEASE know exactly which directive controls your specific case and thoroughly review the portions and guidelines that are applicable to your own unique situation. Security clearance applicants will be instructed which directive and law control their respective cases. This new directive still states about one-third of the way down DoD directive "number 5220.6, January 2, 1992 administrative reissuance incorporating through change for April 20, 1999." The top right-hand corner of this new document states: "This version of DoD directive 5220.6 contains the revised national security adjudicative guidelines used by the director of national intelligence, which are effective for any adjudication on or after June 8, 2017."

I have reviewed this new updated directive for any adjudication on or after June 8, 2017, and this additional chapter will focus on the changes from this new directive as compared to the old one. In sum, the changes are slight, but I do want to point them out.

Changes in New Directive Effective for Any Adjudication on or After June 8, 2017

Page 22 of the new directive states, "It must be noted that the adjudicative process is predicated upon individuals providing relevant information pertaining to their background and character for use in investigating and adjudicating their national security eligibility. Any incident of intentional material falsification or purposeful non-cooperation with security processing is of significant concern. Such conduct raises questions about an individual's judgment, reliability, and trustworthiness and may be predictive of their willingness or ability to protect the national security."

What this paragraph makes crystal clear is that any misstatement or falsification during the process, especially the SF 86, is frowned upon in even harder terms than the earlier directive.

Guideline A – page 23. This directive under Allegiance to the United States notes that "there is no positive test for allegiance, but there are negative indicators. These include participation in or support for acts against the United States or placing the welfare or interests of another country above those of the United States. Finally, the failure to adhere to the laws of the United States to be relevant if the violation of the law is harmful to stated U.S. interests. An individual who engages in acts against the United States or provides support or encouragement to those who do has already demonstrated willingness to compromise national security.

Compared to the old directive, this change to Guideline A makes it broader as far as negative indicators reflecting that someone does not have allegiance to the United States, which could then be problematic, of course, from a security clearance standpoint.

Guideline C – page 26. This entire guideline under foreign preference has been changed. Here is the new Guideline C information under foreign preference.

The Concern. When an individual acts in such a way as to indicate a preference for a foreign country over the United States, then he or she may provide information or make decisions that are harmful to the interests of the United States. Foreign involvement raises concerns about an individual's judgment, reliability, and trustworthiness when it is in conflict with U.S. national interests or when the individual acts to conceal it. *By itself,* the fact that a U.S. citizen is also a citizen of another country is not disqualifying without an objective showing of such conflict or attempt at concealment. The same is true for a U.S. citizen's exercise of any right or privilege of foreign citizenship and any action to acquire or obtain recognition of a foreign citizenship.

Conditions that could raise a security concern and may be disqualifying include:

(a) applying for and/or acquiring citizenship in any other country;

(b) failure to report, or fully disclose when required, to an appropriate security official, the possession of a passport or identity card issued by any country other than the United States;

(c) failure to use a U.S. passport when entering or exiting the U.S.;

(d) participation in foreign activities, including but not limited to:

(1) assuming or attempting to assume any type of employment, position, or political office in a foreign government or military organization; and

(2) otherwise acting to serve the interests of a foreign person, group, organization, or government in any way that conflicts with U.S. national security interests;

(e) using foreign citizenship to protect financial or business interests in another country in violation of U.S. law; and

(f) an act of expatriation from the United States, such as declaration of intent to renounce U.S. citizenship, whether through words or actions.

Conditions that could mitigate security concerns include:

(a) the foreign citizenship is not in conflict with U.S. national security interests;

(b) dual citizenship is based solely on parental citizenship or birth in a foreign country, and there is no evidence of foreign preference;

(c) the individual has expressed a willingness to renounce the foreign citizenship that is in conflict with U.S. national security interests;

(d) the exercise of the rights, privileges, or obligations of foreign citizenship occurred before the individual became a U.S. citizen;

(e) the exercise of the entitlements or benefits of foreign citizenship do not present a national security concern;

(f) the foreign preference, if detected, involves a foreign country, entity, or association that poses a low national security risk;

(g) civil employment or military service was authorized under U.S. law, or the employment or service was otherwise consented to as required by U.S. law; and

(h) any potentially disqualifying activity took place after receiving the approval by the agency head or designee.

Guideline D – page 28. This is the guideline for sexual behavior. The change specifically references that concerning sexual behavior includes conduct occurring in person or via audio, visual, electronic, or written transmission. It further states that no adverse inference concerning the standards in this guideline may be raised solely on the basis of an individual's sexual orientation. Under mitigation, it further allows for deeper resolution of a problem where "the individual has successfully completed an appropriate program of treatment, or is currently enrolled in one, has demonstrated ongoing and consistent compliance with the treatment plan, and/or has received a favorable prognosis from a qualified mental health professional indicating the behavior is readily controllable with treatment."

Guideline E – page 29. This is the personal conduct guideline. This change further references that the government will have concerns for someone's refusal or failure, without reasonable cause, to undergo or cooperate with security processing, including but not limited to meeting with the security investigator for subject interview, completing security forms or releases, cooperation with medical or psychological evaluation, or polygraph examination, if authorized and required, while, at the same time, noting that an additional concern is "deliberately providing false or misleading information; or concealing or omitting information concerning relevant facts to an employer, investigator, security official, competent medical or mental professional involved in making a recommendation relevant to national security eligibility determination, or other government representative."

Guideline F – page 32. This is the guideline for financial considerations. With regard to the concern, the directive has been changed to note that "financial distress can also be caused or exacerbated by, and thus can be a possible indicator of, other issues of personnel security concern such as excessive gambling, mental health conditions, substance misuse, or alcohol abuse or dependence. An individual who is financially overextended is at greater risk of having to engage in illegal or otherwise questionable acts to generate funds." With regard to conditions that raise a concern, this guideline also added the following: "consistent spending beyond one's means or frivolous or irresponsible spending which may be indicated by excessive indebtedness, significant negative cash flow, a history of late payments or of non-payment, or other negative financial indicators."

Under this same guideline, the mitigation was changed and improved a little, specifically under (b) on page 33. "The conditions that resulted in the financial problem were largely beyond the person's control (e.g., loss of employment, a business downturn, unexpected medical emergency, a death, divorce, or separation, clear victimization by predatory lending practices, or identity theft), and the individual acted responsibly under the circumstances." Paragraph (c) was also changed under this guideline as follows: "the individual has received or is receiving financial counseling for the problem from a legitimate and credible source, such as a non-profit credit counseling service, and there are clear indications that the problem is being resolved or is under control." Importantly, with regard to back taxes, paragraph (g) was added for mitigation insofar as "the individual has made arrangements with the appropriate tax authority to file or pay the amount owed and is in compliance with those arrangements."

Guideline G – page 34. This is the guideline for alcohol consumption. A new concern was added that the government will look at under 22(b) as follows: "alcohol-related incidents at work, such as reporting for work or duty in an intoxicated or impaired condition, drinking on the job, or jeopardizing the welfare and safety of others, regardless of whether the individual is diagnosed with alcohol use disorder." Another concern has also been added under (e) as follows: "the failure to follow treatment advice once diagnosed."

Guideline H – page 36. This is now called Drug Involvement and Substance Misuse. The concern has been changed in this guideline to read as follows: "The illegal use of controlled substances, to include the misuse of prescription and non-prescription drugs, and the use of other substances that cause physical or mental impairment or are used in a manner inconsistent with their intended purpose can raise questions about an individual's reliability and trustworthiness, both because such behavior may lead to physical or psychological impairment and because it raises concerns about a person's ability or unwillingness to comply with laws, rules, and regulations. *Controlled substance* means any 'controlled substance' as defined in 21 U.S.C. 802. *Substance misuse* is the generic term adopted in this guideline to describe any of the behaviors listed above."

Guideline I – page 38. This is the guideline for psychological conditions. The concerns were changed here in three parts. Under section 28(a), it now states that "behavior that casts doubt on an individual's judgment, stability, reliability, or trustworthiness, not covered under any other guideline and that may indicate emotional, mental, or personality condition, including, but not limited to, irresponsible, violent, self-harm, suicidal, paranoid, manipulative, impulsive, chronic lying, deceitful, exploitive, or bizarre behaviors." Under (c) it also addresses as a concern "voluntary or involuntary inpatient hospitalization." Finally, another change in the concern is under (e), "pathological gambling, the associated behaviors of which may include unsuccessful attempts to stop gambling, gambling for increasingly higher stakes, usually in an attempt to cover losses; concealing gambling losses; borrowing or stealing money to fund gambling or pay gambling debt; and family conflict resulting from gambling."

Guideline J – page 40. This is the guideline that relates to criminal conduct. A new concern was added, (a), that allows for "a pattern of minor offenses, any one of which on its own would be unlikely to affect a national security eligibility decision, but which in combination cast doubt on the individual's judgment, reliability, or trustworthiness." Another concern was added which is important for prior military service members, under (e), "a discharge or dismissal from the Armed Forces for reasons less than 'Honorable.'"

Guideline K – page 42. This is the guideline regarding handling protected information. Under this guideline, additional mitigation has been added: under (c), "the security violations were due to improper or inadequate training or unclear instructions" and (d), "the violation was inadvertent, it was promptly reported, there was no evidence of compromise, and it does not suggest a pattern."

Guideline M – page 45. Guideline M relates to the use of information technology. Additional mitigation was added under (d), citing the "misuse was due to improper or inadequate training or unclear instructions."

Finally, two additional appendices have been added that were not in the previous directive. To make it simple and clear, the new Appendix B, which is the bond amendment guidance, and Appendix C, the exceptions, are listed in their entirety.

APPENDIX B

BOND AMENDMENT GUIDANCE

On 28 January 2008, Congress amended the IRTPA of 2004, adding statutory restrictions on certain eligibility determinations and establishing waiver and congressional reporting requirements. These modifications are collectively referred to as the "Bond Amendments" and were made effective on 1 January 2008.[6] For the reasons identified in paragraph E.2 above, application of the Bond Amendment's statutory restrictions will be applied to all adjudications covered under this Directive.

1. PROHIBITION: Heads of agencies are prohibited from granting or renewing national security eligibility for any covered individual who is an unlawful user of a controlled substance or is an addict as defined below. If an authorized adjudicative agency has a case pending review that involves an unlawful user of a controlled substance or an addict, the statutory prohibition must be applied and the individual will receive the agency's established administrative review procedures. A meritorious waiver may not be authorized with reference to this prohibition. For purposes of this prohibition:

    (a) an "addict" is any individual who habitually uses any narcotic drug so as to endanger the public morals, health, safety, or welfare; or is so far addicted to the use of narcotic drugs as to

[6] IRTPA of 2004 § 3002, 50 U.S.C. § 3343

have lost the power of self-control with reference to his addiction.

(b)   a "controlled substance" means any "controlled substance" as defined in 21 U.S.C. 802.

2.   **DISQUALIFICATION:** The Bond Amendment also contains disqualification provisions which apply only to those covered individuals seeking access to Sensitive Compartmented Information (SCI), Special Access Programs (SAP), or Restricted Data (RD). Heads of agencies may not grant or renew access to SCI, SAP, or RD to a covered individual who:

(a)   has been convicted in any court of the U.S. of a crime, was sentenced to imprisonment for a term exceeding one year, and was incarcerated as a result of that sentence for not less than one year;

(b)   has been discharged or dismissed from the Armed Forces under dishonorable conditions; or

(c)   is determined to be mentally incompetent; an individual is "mentally incompetent" when he or she has been declared mentally incompetent as determined by competency proceedings conducted in a court or administrative agency with proper jurisdiction.

3.   **WAIVER STANDARD AND PROCEDURES:** When a disqualifier reflected in paragraph 2(a) – (c) above exists, the adjudicator will proceed with the adjudication using the appropriate mitigation conditions found in these adjudicative guidelines. If the adjudicator would have had a favorable decision but for the Bond Amendment disqualification, a meritorious waiver may be appropriate.

(a)   Meritorious waivers will be considered an "Exception" to the adjudicative guidelines and will be annotated as a "Waiver" in the adjudicative decision recorded in the appropriate databases listed in para. E.5. Adjudicators will provide a detailed justification for the meritorious waiver in the final adjudicative report.

(b) If, after applying the appropriate mitigating factors listed in these adjudicative guidelines, a meritorious waiver is not appropriate, the SCI, SAP, or RD access will be denied or revoked with a written explanation that cites the adjudicative guidelines applied and the Bond Amendment disqualifier. The authorized adjudicative agency's established administrative review procedures shall be followed in all such cases.

(c) Each authorized adjudicative agency shall maintain a record of the number and type of meritorious waivers granted, to include the rationale for each waiver, and shall report this data annually to the SecEA in advance of the annual report to Congress. Authorized adjudicative agencies will also maintain a record of all disqualifications, broken down by type, due to Bond Amendment requirements.

4. Authorized adjudicative agencies often have no ability to predict whether the covered individual for whom national security eligibility determinations are being made will also require access to SCI, SAP, or RD. Accordingly, the following guidance applies to all national security adjudicative determinations:

(a) All adjudicators will determine whether any of the Bond Amendment disqualifiers in paragraphs 2(a) – (c) apply to the case being adjudicated.

(b) If a disqualifier exists, adjudicators shall annotate that fact in one of the databases identified in paragraph E.5 to ensure that any subsequent requests for access to SCI, SAP, or RD for the individual will undergo appropriate re-adjudication and waiver procedures in meritorious cases.

APPENDIX C

EXCEPTIONS

Exceptions are an adjudicative decision to grant initial or continued eligibility for access to classified information or to hold a sensitive position despite failure to meet the full adjudicative or investigative standards. The authorized exceptions are defined below and supersede the definitions in Office of Management and Budget memorandum, *Reciprocal Recognition of Existing Personnel Security Clearances*, 14 November 2007.

Waiver (W):

> Eligibility granted or continued despite the presence of substantial issue information that would normally preclude eligibility. Approval authorities may approve a waiver only when the benefit of initial or continued eligibility clearly outweighs any security concerns. A waiver may also require conditions for eligibility as described below.

Condition (C):

> Eligibility granted or continued, despite the presence of issue information that can be partially but not completely mitigated with the provision that additional security measures shall be required to mitigate the issue(s). Such measures include, but are not limited to, additional security monitoring, access restrictions, submission of

periodic financial statements, or attendance at counseling sessions.

Deviation (D):

Eligibility granted or continued despite either a significant gap in coverage or scope of the investigations. "Significant gap" for this purpose means either compete lack of coverage for a period of six months or longer within the most recent five years investigated or the lack of one or more relevant investigative scope components (e.g., employment checks, financial review, or a subject interview) in its entirety.

Out of Scope (O):

Reinvestigation is overdue.

Conclusion

I hope that you have found this information helpful and useful. At a minimum, this book should serve as a starting point for any question you have about security clearance issues, problems, concerns, denials, and revocations. This book is for informational purposes only and should not be construed as specific legal advice, as every individual situation is different and the advice may change depending upon the facts of each situation. I advise people to use this as general information and to seek the advice of a qualified attorney of their own choosing to review the specific facts of their own unique situation. If you need my assistance, please do not hesitate to contact me.

www.BondandBotes.com

www.SecurityClearanceDefenseLawyer.com

Important Information! Please note that the information in this book covers and relies on the government's use of DOD Directive 5220.6, which contains the revised adjudicative guidelines implemented for the Department of Defense by the Under Secretary of Defense for Intelligence on August 30, 2006 and made effective for any adjudication in which a statement of reasons is issued on or after September 1, 2006. **If you are looking at any other directive with a different date or number, then some or all of the information contained in this book may**

not apply or be correct as to your situation. Also, carefully read Chapter 9 of this book, which discusses the new directive effective for any adjudication on or after June 8, 2017!

Additionally, the information in this book covers and relies on the government's use of the Standard Form 86 revised December 2010. If you are looking at any other Standard Form 86 with a date other than December 2010, then some or all of the information contained in this book may not apply or be correct as to your situation.

www.ingramcontent.com/pod-product-compliance
Lightning Source LLC
Chambersburg PA
CBHW061513180526
45171CB00001B/167